The God Idea

How one idea can change the world!

By Musekiwa Samuriwo

African Knight Publications

Harare, Zimbabwe.

The God Idea

Originally published in English under the title "**The God Idea**" series by Musekiwa Samuriwo

DTP - African Knight Productions
Cover design – African Knight Productions
Front and Back Cover photograph "the head of invention" sculpted by Sir Eduardo Paolozzi (1989) – photographed by Rudo Nyangulu
http://ethos-photographic.blogspot.com/

Consulting Editor – Rumbidzai O. Phiri

ISBN: 978-0-7974—4593-2

Scripture quotations are from The Holy Bible Revised Standard Version copyright© 1946, 1952 by Division of Christian Education of the National Council of the Churches of Christ in the United States printed by Collins Clear Type Press

Other scripture quotations are taken from Amplified Bible, Copyright © 1954, 1958, 1962, 1964, 1965, 1987bt The Lockman Foundation. All rights Reserved used by permission.

♡Art
of being humane

The book supports cancer awareness and other charity initiatives in Zimbabwe through The Art of Being Humane.

This book supports orphans and vulnerable children through ARK (Art Reach Kids)

Acknowledgments

To our Father in Heaven, to Jesus the Author and the Finisher of my faith and to the Holy Spirit the Wonderful Counselor who leads me into all truth. To those who have helped to shape my thoughts in relation to this book, David Chifunyise, Douglas Hlatwayo, Sifiso Madhovi, Shingai Kuwaza, Bargely Makumbe and Kumbukani Phiri over hours of rambling and minutes of discussion. To those who encouraged me to continue writing even when it didn't make sense namely, Shingi Jangara and to Anthony Dube and Sharon Sevenzo for big dreams and many more. To my family for times when I have been difficult to understand, resembling an ascetic recluse. And to countless others, who've willingly entered my life and shared their faith with me, mentors like Dr Mugaviri, brothers, sisters and the church as a whole. To God be all the glory forever.

"I began by declaring that we live and preach between times. Only a pulpit that identifies with the milieu of the time will be heard over the babble of other voices demanding people's attention. My earlier work on identification and preaching makes clear that identifying with the postmodern world does not mean prima facie acceptance or rejection of its values or worldview. Creating identification means taking the postmodern world seriously and addressing it from a collaborative rather than adversarial stance. A postmodern world demands a pulpit willing to be a viable conversation partner. In the words of one evangelical scholar, "The challenge for the church is to claim this postmodern context for Christ." Preaching that recognizes and addresses the shifting idioms offers the world timeless good news of God's grace, love and provision."

(From Apologetic Preaching © 2000 by Craig A. Localzo. **Published** by InterVarsity Press. All rights reserved. Used with Permission)

Preface

Ironically, this book in many ways reflects the contents and discussions of the book itself. It is the culmination of years of searching and asking God concerning one of the most misunderstood and often desired aspects of human endeavour; creativity. For at least eight years, I've shared passionately on the subject of creativity and the power of ideas in communities.

Yet, I've often found that it is a subject many aren't keen to talk about or it is often not considered an important subject among the major themes of Christian living. In some quarters creativity has even been frowned upon and looked at as the disease of the struggling artist or the rebellious 'secular' artist or atheist scientist who hates God. Yet, ideas themselves are inescapable and have over the years shaped and defined our lives and societies as a whole.

The world has been shaped by the thoughts and conceptions of an individual seeking to 'try' out something different and to challenge the status quo. When William Blake an English poet from the 18th and 19th century says, "What is now proved was once only imagined." he captures something significant. When we look around and consider theories and human enterprise like driving a car, it was all once an unproved idea locked up in the mind of an individual.

So it is with great intent that I've sought to write a book on the power of ideas.

More importantly, this book is designed to challenge believers on the impact of God's intentions and ideas on society. This book isn't about 'heaven storming' creativity and ideas but rather it's about 'earth storming' ideas. It is a book that considers what happens when earth is invaded by God Ideas.

So often we know it, we walk in the understanding that the power of God dwells in us. But for some of us, that power is limited to church meetings and 'spiritual' activity. Rarely does the Holy Spirit impact the mundane or 'secular'.

This book seeks to encourage what I'm calling the God Idea. The God idea is something we may consider to be the inherent calling on every believer to, "...do mighty exploits for God." (Dan 11:32b RSV)

It is the God idea that inspired Joseph and provided him with the strategy to help Egypt survive 7 years of famine. It is the God idea that liberated the Israelites as Moses spoke to Pharaoh. It is the God idea that came in the fullness of Christ Jesus to gather all things to Him who is deserving of all glory.

My desire in writing this book, is to inspire believers to humbly surrender to God, so as to unlock their God given potential that overcomes Satan and the gates of

Hades (see Matt16:18 RSV) and works to bring about God's will to the nations.

Exciting and explosive, will be the work of God in Christians who are willing and obedient to fulfill their calling in Christ.

The God idea is significant. It is what God called you and me for. I believe that through grace, every believer is in possession of God's CREATIVE power that raised Christ from the dead. Every believer is in possession of gifts and talents that can be used to bring about the transformation and revival of nations. Whatever the sphere, from politics, health, to entertainment and recreation; there are believers who have a God idea that serves to exalt the name of Christ and helps to redeem cultures.

It is important that believers all over the world consider seriously what Craig Localzo a pastor and writer says in the quote *pg 4* that, "...we need to win over this postmodern era we live in for Christ." We must boldly proclaim Christ in the church, in the marketplaces, in the halls of politics and governance and in the fields and confines of recreation and entertainment. Amid the chatter of countless voices and ideas demanding people's attention we need 'earth storming' creative ideas that identify and challenge the status quo to and for the glory of God.

Let us embark together on an interesting journey of discovery into the wealth of riches God has prepared for us in Christ Jesus. Our careers, our families, our schools and our nations will be different when we humbly accept the will of God in our lives and pursue the God idea within us with much zeal and wisdom.

This is my prayer for the world, that God's kingdom come and that His will be done on earth as it is in heaven.

Amen.

Contents

Table of Figures

Chapter 1.

What is a God Idea?

How great are thy works, O Lord! Thy thoughts are very deep! Psa 92:5 RSV

At the very foundation of human society, there is a key unit of development that affects every aspect of existence. It is called the idea. The Concise Oxford Dictionary (2001) defines an idea as,

> Ideas form the basis of all human endeavours. Someone somewhere conceived something and sought to make it a reality.

- **n:** A thought or suggestion as to a possible course of action. ➢ a mental impression. ➢ a belief.
- – ORIGIN ME: via L. from Gk *idea* 'form, pattern', from the base of *idein* 'to see'.

At various stages in human civilization, countless individuals have sought to understand their surroundings and provide answers or solutions to some prevailing problems.

Invention, as with design has contributed to a number of advances human beings have made throughout history.

Clearly, it must also be appreciated that ideas have driven humanity to do some of the vilest things we can imagine and some of the most amazing things we can conceive. And these ideas have had an effect in 4 distinct ways on history. *The first 3 adapted from Hein Van Wyk (2006).*

- **Horizontal:** Ideas have traveled around the globe, from one geographical area to another.
- **Vertical:** Ideas have diffused into cultures through different classes of people.
- **Temporal:** Ideas have consistently been passed on to future generations.
- **Eternal:** ideas have had an impact on eternity.

Yet, beyond the ideas of man, God has also had plans and ideas for what He created. From the very foundations of creation, God had intentions for His creation especially human beings.

It is His interaction with humanity that has provided some of the most insightful and transformational ideas that have contributed to the betterment of society. These ideas are often a result of what Napoleon Hill author of the book Think and Grow Rich calls Creative imagination, when the finite mind of man has direct communication with the Infinite Intelligence.

Napoleon Hill talks about 12 principles of true riches without mention of God but the real intent and source of creative imagination that is; the God Idea is to give glory to God and to present His will to nations.

So importantly, a God idea is when God's intentions permeate creation and society and affect and influence the order of the day (when the finite draws on the infinite).

From men like Abraham in the Bible to inspirational scientists like George Washington Carver Jr, God has been involved in inspiring creativity and ultimately providing innovation. The God Idea is essentially derived from our understanding of the will of God. As much as human beings have intentions, the God idea is when individuals, communities and nations surrender their intentions and allow God's will to pervade society with understanding and transformational wisdom. The God idea is what God knows and what He wants us to know and to do.

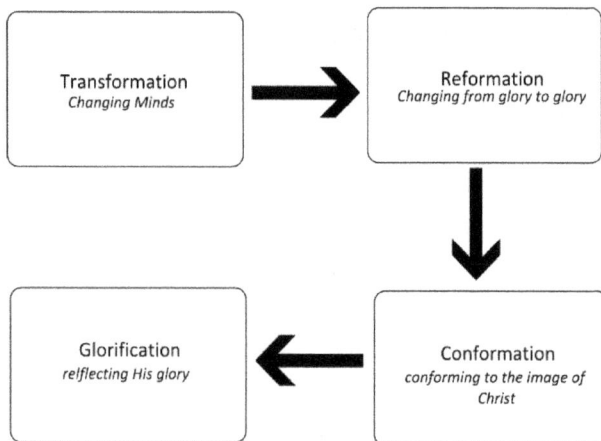

Transformation
Changing Minds

Reformation
Changing from glory to glory

Glorification
relflecting His glory

Conformation
conforming to the image of Christ

Figure 1 Ideas that glorify God

14

At the very core, God's involvement in a community or individual is redemptive, that is to say it reclaims what may have been considered dead or destroyed.

A God idea thus becomes a skill, insight, talent or a combination thereof that serves to benefit the user and other people (community or nation) to the glory of God.

Figure 1 adapted from Hein Van Wyk (2006) above shows the levels we transcend when someone continues to pursue the God idea. We experience

- **Transformation**: a total change in form, shape and character,
- **Reformation**: being restored to God's original intentions
- **Conformation** – living to the patterns and standards of the kingdom of God.

Expectedly, there is a concerted progression towards glorification when we perfectly reflect the glory of God.

I believe, it is important to emphasize that God ideas arise out of a number of Christian fundamentals which we will look at in later chapters;

- **Faith** – total assurance of things that are unseen.
- **Humility** – total surrender to the will and power of God.
- **Wisdom** – reverence of the Lord. Fearing him in worship and awe.
- **Grace** – unmerited and underserved favour.

- **Trust** – the ability to continue accepting that God is control when things remain unclear and uncertain.
- **Perseverance** - resolute pursuit of a desired goal.
- **Vision** – a picture or glimpse of the future.

These fundamentals are important to consider when God is involved in bringing about transformation in an individual, community, nations or generations.

In essence, whenever God involves Himself in His creation, it is inevitable that the idea will transcend all expectations and surpass temporal history in significance.

Much like our pursuit of a biblical worldview according to Walsh and Middelton (pg 33, 1984) a God Idea will breach all barriers known to human society from cultural, economic and political. *(See Figure 2 below)*

God ideas were evident in people who lived in Biblical times and are evident now, in the people who live in this modern age because the Holy Spirit now dwells in our hearts (Rom 5:5 RSV). There are God ideas resident in believers all over the world for the times we are living in.

Whether we consider the persecuted church or the 'liberated' church, God is inspiring Christians all over the world to make a stand for Him and to bring about revival and reformation.

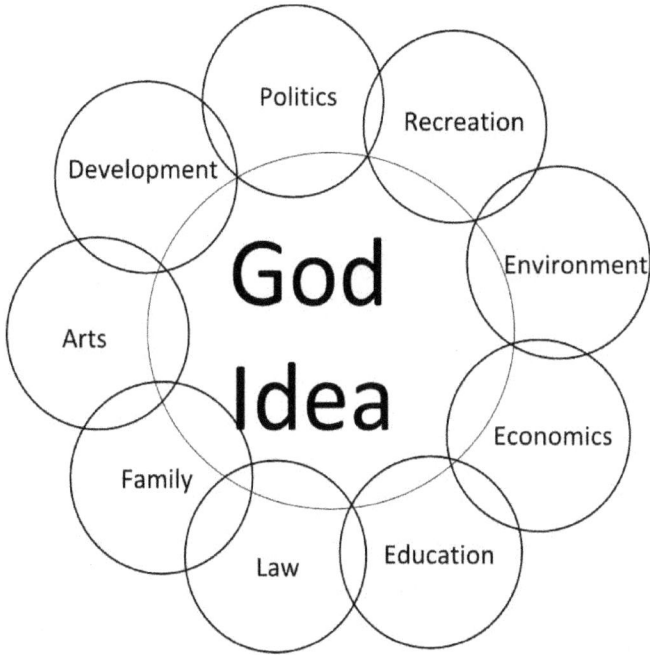

Figure 2 God Ideas spreading

Chapter 2.

God ideas in the Old Testament

In the Old Testament we can truly uncover a wealth of insight into God ideas that pervaded a society and contributed to its transformation and salvation.

At the very inception of time we learn that God made the heavens and the earth. We learn through Genesis 1 that God was intent on creating something in His likeness. It is here that we see that God created man in His image (Gen 1:26 RSV). God had specific intentions for man as His direct reflection and representation on earth.

Firstly, man was to serve God as a steward responsible for maintaining and cultivating the earth. We also know that Adam was given instruction to work, to subdue the elements of the earth and to have dominion over them. Furthermore, Adam was to grow and multiply and fill the earth.

In these references we uncover that man had a unique and distinct mandate from God. (Genesis 2:19-21 RSV) also reveals something profound about God's unique creation called man.

The Brand Specialist

Gen 2:19-21

19 So out of the ground the Lord God formed every beast of the field and every bird of the air, and brought them to the man to see what he would call them; and whatever the man called every living creature, that was its name. 20 The man gave names to all cattle, and to the birds of the air, and to every beast of the field; but for the man there was not found a helper fit for him. RSV

This verse helps us unpack and appreciate something unique and excitedly different that's inherent in man and not in any other

> Key
>
> We are uniquely created by God to subdue the earth.

animal or beast in creation. What these three verses reveal is a sort of 'co-labouring' relationship between God and man.

Firstly, we can establish that God through His original creative power had created all the living things. Creation is our first encounter in the Bible of God's original creative power and ideas.

It is evident from scripture that God's creativity is above and beyond any given or known natural law because all the creatures in their explicit diversity and uniqueness were formed out of nothing.

Secondly, God in full appreciation of the mandate he had bestowed on man (Gen 1:26-27 RSV), then provides

19

the platform for Adam to display the capacity he had been endowed with by God. As we read the text, we can discover that Adam was granted a level of intelligence and analytical skills.

In a bid to establish and affirm His word, God presented the animals to Adam and granted him the opportunity to establish authority over the animals by naming them.

Adam became the brand specialist, someone capable of recognizing, naming and establishing identity for the animals God had created. If we presume that Adam was using an ancient language, we can still appreciate that each animal was named according to its inherent and exhibited characteristics.

Adam recognized these attributes and was also uniquely intertwined with God to understand and appreciate all that God had made.

In some implied respects, this narrative gives us an appreciation of the depth of imaging and consequent unity that was between God and His unique and intelligent creation. We see this because whatever Adam named the animals, "...that was its name." (Gen 2:19 paraphrase RSV) There was clear understanding between the Creator and His image on earth.

> *God's intent for man at the very beginning was to appreciate what he made, to subdue it and nurture it as an expression of worship.*

Fathers of invention and design

Gen 4:20-22

20 Adah bore Jabal; he was the father of those who dwell in tents and have cattle. 21 His brother's name was Jubal; he was the father of all those who play the lyre and pipe. 22 Zillah bore Tubal-cain; he was the forger of all instruments of bronze and iron. RSV

In later times when man had succumbed to sin we discover that God's intent for man though corrupted was still apparent.

> **Key**
>
> Human beings have the capacity and intelligence to invent.

Jabal, Jubal and Tubal-cain further present to us that there was still something special inherent in sinful man. Adam had fallen from grace and Cain had descended deeper into sin by committing murder.

Yet, what we understand from scripture is that God's redemptive plan was at work directly through Seth and his descendents. We also see that God had already committed to man the ability to subdue the earth.

It is revealed in the reference to these 3 men who specifically represent 3 aspects of human enterprise; agriculture and investment, recreation and artistic expression and scientific endeavour (design and engineering).

Though clearly lacking in piety and righteousness these 3 men carried something in their corruption of what God had given man in creation.

'Studious they appear
Of arts that polish life-inventors rare —
Unmindful of their Maker, though His Spirit
Taught them; but they His gifts acknowledged none.
(MILTON)

Milton puts it beautifully here that, they received this knowledge and ability from their Creator but chose not to acknowledge their Maker in their endeavours. Yet, what we can uncover from other passages in the Old Testament is that there were others who acknowledged God and through their obedience, God responded by giving them diverse skills and abilities.

Unlike these three brothers who are mentioned in Genesis as being rebellious 'originators' of key aspects of human enterprise, characters like Joseph, Nehemiah and Bezalel give us an insight into the impact God ideas have on society. God ideas in these men were a testimony to the existence and glory of God, above the endeavours and ingenuity of man.

God was always intent on being involved in human endeavour and enterprise, but humanity refuses to acknowledge Him in what they do.

Bezalel the skilled and masterful craftsman

Moses, as the leader of Israel at the time, made a bold confession to the people that Bezalel had been selected by God and had received 5 key things. The purpose and function of these abilities was to contribute to the design and construction of the Tabernacle.

> **Key**
>
> God selects individuals to do His work by name.

Unlike the 3 sons of Lamech we find that Bezalel was granted similar skills for a more glorious and righteous work in God. His skills and abilities were the same as Tubal-cain yet within them was something more important; the Spirit of God.

Who was Bezalel?

Bezalel was the son of Uri who in turn was the son of Hur, who was descended from the tribe of Judah. He was someone to whom God had revealed something special and significant, necessary for a tribe dwelling in the wilderness to fully worship God. Bezalel was uniquely gifted by God to do a lot of diverse and creative things.

Ex 31:1-5

The Lord said to Moses, 2 "See, I have called by name Bez'alel the son of Uri, son of Hur, of the tribe of Judah: 3 and I have filled him with the Spirit of God, with ability and intelligence, with knowledge and all craftsmanship, 4 to devise artistic designs, to work in gold, silver, and bronze, 5 in cutting stones for setting, and in carving wood, for work in every craft. RSV

The first thing to establish about God ideas is that God calls someone by name. Much of what God seeks to do through an individual is based on the fact that God calls them.

When God wanted to build the Tabernacle, He told Moses that He had empowered someone. When He wanted to establish His will and purposes on earth He called someone. Bezalel represents a clear picture of God's cultural mandate on earth. In this instance, it is in relation to worship and devotion.

Ex 35:30-35

30 And Moses said to the people of Israel, "See, the Lord has called by name Bez'alel the son of Uri, son of Hur, of the tribe of Judah; 31 and he has filled him with the Spirit of God, with ability, with intelligence, with knowledge, and with all craftsmanship,

32 to devise artistic designs, to work in gold and silver and bronze, 33 in cutting stones for setting, and in carving wood, for work in every skilled craft. 34 And he has inspired him to teach, both him and Oho'liab the son of Ahis'amach of the tribe of Dan.

35 He has filled them with ability to do every sort of work done by a craftsman or by a designer or by an embroiderer in blue and purple and scarlet stuff and

fine twined linen, or by a weaver - by any sort of workman or skilled designer. RSV

The Spirit of God

Also, Moses established that God had chosen Bezalel and He had filled Him with His Spirit. What we understand of the Holy Spirit in the New Testament, is that Jesus left us the Holy Spirit as a guide and counselor (John 14 & 16 RSV).

> Key
>
> Bezalel was filled with the Spirit of God.

Jesus tells us that the Holy Spirit will reveal and guide men into all truth.

We also know that the Spirit empowers and gives gifts to men (1Cor 12). It is amazing to see how much skill and knowledge the Holy Spirit gave Bezalel to endeavour in craftsmanship.

It is evident from this passage that the Spirit of God isn't limited to less tangible spiritual and administrative gifts alone but He is able to give men very practical gifts.

Through Bezalel, we capture a glimpse of God's influence on the life of man on earth. As much as God influences our souls, we see here that the Holy Spirit has influence over our bodies and the labour of our hands. Bezalel as we see from the passage was given skill, ability and knowledge by the Holy Spirit in all kinds of craft. Moses goes on to list the skills that the Spirit of God had given to Bezalel.

Ability

The passage reveals that the Holy Spirit gave Bezalel capacity and skill to function in more practical activities like design and construction.

God the architect of the Tabernacle set about ensuring that the tabernacle He desired would meet His specifications. This He achieved by ensuring that there were individuals who had the necessary aptitude to meet the intended objective. Simply put, God ensured that Bezalel was 'able' to do what was required of him. Bezalel was given the ability to use his hands to make artistic designs in gold, silver and bronze, to cut and set stone, to work in wood and to engage in all kinds of artistic craftsmanship.

Intelligence

God also gave Bezalel the capacity for logic and reasoning in executing his activities. There was a particular requirement for the individual leading the work of designing and constructing the elements that made up the Tabernacle.

Intelligence is synonymous with words like aptitude, acumen, intellect and brains. It is clear here that God ensured that Bezalel also had the acumen to ensure that the work of building the tabernacle was excellent. God's intention in Bezalel was to give us a general view of how human intelligence, intellect and invention can have a God-focused view.

Knowledge

Combined with intelligence Bezalel was also endowed with the necessary information, facts and awareness. God clearly provided Bezalel with expertise to help in the development of the objects that were to contribute to the construction of the tabernacle.

Knowledge plays a significant role in the development and implementation of a God idea. Knowledge represents Bezalel's capacity to assimilate and process data and convert it to a workable process of doing things. Through the power of the Holy Spirit, Bezalel achieved a level of professional realization of different aspects of craftsmanship.

Craftsmanship

Craftsmanship refers to the ability to produce excellent and presentable works. It was necessary for the Tabernacle to be designed according to the blueprint provided by God. Furthermore, it was necessary that though being a shadow of the tabernacle in heaven it would be magnificent to view.

Religion and worship for God are not limited to the songs the Israelites were to sing or acts of prostration, but also in the fact that true devotion to God was to absorb all aspects of human activity including our inventive and aesthetic nature.

Bezalel's ability to shape and mold in wood, metal and other materials was an important ingredient required to display his worship and devotion to God.

Inspiration to teach

Bezlalel was also granted the ability to teach. More than selfishly possessing the work given to him, God ensured that Bezalel was also able to teach others. Knowledge and understanding must be shared. Someone once amended the popular quote, "Knowledge is power." by adding the word 'share', thus implying that shared knowledge is power. It was imperative that Bezalel be skilled in building the necessary artifacts but also that he be able to teach others as well support the saying that, "Many hands make light work."

> *God ideas are not limited in their expression and can be revealed in works of art, design and construction.*

Joseph – the household manager

Joseph who was aptly named by Pharaoh Zaphenath-paneah meaning to some, savior of the age (Gen 41:45) and to others sustainer of life endured countless trials and hardships in his early years growing up.

Yet, he ultimately brought about new management and economic theory to the land of Egypt. This resulted in him being promoted to something equivalent to a modern day prime minister.

As the story goes Joseph was a young boy full of dreams and desires and it was a wonderful gift he had received from God. But dreams of grandeur and glory are often misunderstood and thus Joseph was misunderstood by his family.

Even when the gift or talent is misunderstood by people, it is important to understand that each individual is unique and inherently designed for a specific purpose and function on behalf of God. Joseph was different in many respects to his brothers.

The dreamer

He had ambition beyond his current context (he courageously or arrogantly shared his dreams with his brothers and parents.)

Joseph had the capacity to visualize the future in dreams. The story goes that when he was about 17 years old, Joseph had a dream where he and his other brothers were binding sheaves in the field. To his brothers disdain Joseph then shared that his sheaf arose and stood upright whilst their sheaves gathered around his and bowed.

> Key
>
> Courageously believing in the dreams God gives us, is a key ingredient to establishing God ideas.

Young and somewhat naïve, Joseph unwittingly shared his dreams of the future with his family and was inevitably misunderstood and disliked for his ambition. But one thing was certain that in Joseph, God had raised a dreamer with the inherent ability to see the future. I'm instantly reminded of a poem written by a man or woman called anonymous,

To laugh is to risk appearing the fool.
To place our ideas, our dreams, before a crowd is to risk their loss.
To live is to risk dying.

To hope is to risk despair. To try is to risk failure.
The person who risks nothing, does nothing, as nothing,
and is nothing.
Only a person who risks is free.
—Anonymous

This poem captures a reflection of what I believe Joseph was like. Joseph was a person brimming with hope and thus he was venturesome and full of courage and adventure. He would have been a person willing to take the risk. In respect of the information we have about him in scripture, Joseph was willing to share his ideas and dreams with his family.

Father's favourite

Joseph was also an individual caught between a rock and hard place, having the favour and love of his father and the contempt of his brothers. Simply put Joseph was 'daddy's favourite', the 'spoilt' one in the family.

The inevitable result of this 'dysfunctional' family situation was that Joseph was nearly killed. But, by God's favour and the mercy of one of his brothers, Joseph was sold off as a slave and found himself in the land of Egypt.

Ominous as the thought of slavery would've been, Joseph was on the path towards fulfilling what he had been born to do. From the caravan of the Ishmaelite slave merchants, Joseph found himself in Potiphar's house.

Joseph proved effective and diligent to such an extent that Potiphar's house prospered because of him. This not only courted his promotion but unwanted interest from Potiphar's wife. As the story goes, Joseph was accused of rape and was confined to prison for a number of years.

After the years of affliction and hardship Joseph's opportunity beckoned when Pharaoh was distressed by two dreams which neither he nor his wise men and political advisors could understand. It was at this moment that a young foreigner with a dream, a criminal record and no understanding of Egyptian economics and politics became the wise advisor...

> Gen 41:32-43
> 32 And the doubling of Pharaoh's dream means that the thing is fixed by God, and God will shortly bring it to pass. RSV

One of the first things Joseph did after explaining the meaning of the dreams was to explain why Pharaoh had had the two dreams. It was because God had made a firm decision to bring about famine in the land of Egypt and that it was going to happen soon.

God Ideas are based on the truth that God is about a work and He wants to involve His people in whatever He's doing (Amos 3:7). At the very beginning of the process of transformation and redemption God through Joseph provides a solution for the problem...

33 Now therefore let Pharaoh select a man discreet and wise, and set him over the land of Egypt. 34 Let Pharaoh proceed to appoint overseers over the land, and take the fifth part of the produce of the land of Egypt during the seven plenteous years.

35 And let them gather all the food of these good years that are coming, and lay up grain under the authority of Pharaoh for food in the cities, and let them keep it. 36 That food shall be a reserve for the land against the seven years of famine which are to befall the land of Egypt, so that the land may not perish through the famine." RSV

Joseph proceeded to provide Pharaoh with counsel and strategy to mitigate the imminent crisis. There are four things Joseph recommends to Pharaoh,

- **Leadership (Governor)** – Joseph proposed that Pharaoh elect a man who would be capable of handling a lot or pressure, namely managing the future of Egypt's economic and social well being. He was to be a discreet (careful in speech so as to draw to much attention) and wise (capable of good judgement and having knowledge and experience)
- **Administrators (commissioners)** – beneath the governor, there were to be commissioners who were to serve the express purpose of ensuring that a fifth of all the harvest in the land was collected.
- **Grain storage management** in the seven years of plenty to ensure that Egypt would survive the seven years of famine.
- **Strategic reserves** in the cities where they would be monitored and managed best.

This Joseph iterates was so that, "The country may not be ruined by the famine."

> 37 This proposal seemed good to Pharaoh and to all his servants. 38 And Pharaoh said to his servants, "Can we find such a man as this, in whom is the Spirit of God?" RSV

With a clear understanding of the plan, Pharaoh's recommendation and leadership prescribed that such a godly man filled with the spirit of God be found. It is interesting to note how a 'secular' king had clear understanding of what was required in the given circumstance and his enquiries led to someone with unique abilities. Pharaoh naturally in light of all he'd heard and seen made a viable and wise decision...

> 39 So Pharaoh said to Joseph, "Since God has shown you all this, there is none so discreet and wise as you are; 40 you shall be over my house, and all my people shall order themselves as you command; only as regards the throne will I be greater than you." RSV

At this point, Joseph had just been released from prison (where he was serving his term for a rape he didn't commit).

He was a foreigner, who had no place advising the king on national policy especially in a time of distress and potential crisis. He also didn't have the expertise to manage a nation; he had managed households and a prison.

Yet, there seemed no better candidate than Joseph for the vacant post that Pharaoh had created to ensure that the impending national crisis would be averted.

> 41 And Pharaoh said to Joseph, "Behold, I have set you over all the land of Egypt." 42 Then Pharaoh took his signet ring from his hand and put it on Joseph's hand, and arrayed him in garments of fine linen, and put a gold chain about his neck;
>
> 43 and he made him to ride in his second chariot; and they cried before him, "Bow the knee!" Thus he set him over all the land of Egypt. RSV

This becomes an important milestone in the history of a nation. Pharaoh was struggling to understand his dream which had national and international consequences. He needed someone to help him understand what was at stake.

So when Joseph was able to interpret Pharaoh's dreams, he was given a position of influence. From being rejected and sold into slavery, to being falsely accused and forgotten in jail, Joseph becomes the second most powerful man in Egypt entrusted by Pharaoh with the responsibility of steering the whole nation through a time of potential difficulty.

Importantly, what God works in Joseph in modern times may be referred to as a combination of management frameworks. One of great importance is scenario planning. Others of note are disaster management and business continuity.

Gen 41:44-45

44 Moreover Pharaoh said to Joseph, "I am Pharaoh, and without your consent no man shall lift up hand or foot in all the land of Egypt." 45 And Pharaoh called Joseph's name Zaph'enath-pane'ah; and he gave him in marriage As'enath, the daughter of Poti'phera priest of On. So Joseph went out over the land of Egypt. RSV

Pharaoh makes a bold proclamation of his faith and deference to Joseph by giving him authority to direct the political and economic affairs of Egypt and by conferring him with a name that is sometimes interpreted as savior of the age or sustainer of life. It is remarkable how a young Hebrew boy who was a dreamer is then recognized in 'his land of affliction' as the saviour of the age or sustainer of life because he obediently continued doing what he believed God wanted him to do, dreaming and interpreting dreams.

> *Joseph's story shows us that God ideas work through individuals and ultimately, that one individual can bring transformation to a whole nation.*

Joshua – Military Strategist

Josh 6:1

> Now Jericho was shut up from within and from without because of the people of Israel; none went out, and none came in. RSV

The Israelites had miraculously been rescued by God from the onslaught of vengeful Egyptians and they were gradually becoming a nation. Jericho was to be an important milestone in their venture to be established in the land of Canaan.

> **Key**
>
> Obedience means responding to God's instruction, even when it doesn't seem to make sense.

Hence, with a reputation of defeating the chariots of Pharaoh they approached the fortified oasis city with fertile fields and year round flowing springs. How were they going to overcome this city that stood between them and the promised lands of Canaan? The natural and obvious answer would be a siege.

The siege of Jericho should be considered as one of the shortest and most peculiar sieges in military history that lasted seven days. It's also recorded that the attacking force had no casualties and the besieged were comprehensively defeated.

It presented a unique offensive attack of walking around the wall and singing worship songs. There were no siege works or large cannons and inventions of war.

There are many respected military strategists in history from Hannibal Barca of Carthage, Julius Caesar, Winston Churchill, Shaka the Zulu and so on but for many of these, their offensive attacks inevitably resulted in large casualties of their own armies.

There is even one named Pyrrhus from whom we get the word pyrrhic which refers to a victory achieved by so great a cost that it proves not to be worthwhile. Yet, Joshua gives us a glimpse of a man who understood that God was the ultimate strategist in all respects.

Prior to the siege, Joshua was assessing the field of his first battle, when he saw a man standing aside from him with his sword unsheathed. Curious and courageous Joshua challenged the man by asking, "Whose side are you on?"

The man's response to any soldier would have been worrisome if not scary. The man responded saying, "Neither, but as the Captain of the Lord's army I have come." Instantly, Joshua knew that he had encountered someone of greater and superior significance.

His concurrent submission and worship reveals something of great importance, as it changed the face, reality and outcome of the battle that was to come. What we then see is a man who submits to God's peculiar siege strategy.

Josh 6:2-5

2 And the Lord said to Joshua, "See, I have given into your hand Jericho, with its king and mighty men of valor. 3 You shall march around the city, all the men of war going around the city once. Thus shall you do for six days. 4 And seven priests shall bear seven trumpets of rams' horns before the ark; and on the seventh day you shall march around the city seven times, the priests blowing the trumpets.

5 And when they make a long blast with the ram's horn, as soon as you hear the sound of the trumpet, then all the people shall shout with a great shout; and the wall of the city will fall down flat, and the people shall go up every man straight before him." RSV

It may have seemed foolish in the eyes of both Israel and its enemies but Joshua was certain of something, that whatever the Captain of the Host would command he would do.

Josh 6:6-7

6 So Joshua the son of Nun called the priests and said to them, "Take up the ark of the covenant, and let seven priests bear seven trumpets of rams' horns before the ark of the Lord." 7 And he said to the people, "Go forward; march around the city, and let the armed men pass on before the ark of the Lord." RSV

It is also significant to note that the siege of Jericho was not only a military undertaking but also a religious one, as the trumpets blown by the priests were jubilee trumpets used to make a bold proclamation that the God of heaven and earth was involved in the doom of the city.

Ultimately, the walls of Jericho, "...came tumbling down," and Israel with the help of God's peculiar strategy wrested the oasis city and gained strategic reserves that would facilitate the advancing of the people into Canaan's interior lands.

Furthermore, they attained a significant victory that sent a message to the other tribal cities and kingdoms in the land of Canaan that the Captain of the Lord's host had come.

> *Joshua reveals to us that God ideas are necessary in the strategic endeavours of a nation.*

Nehemiah – the builder

Project management 101

There have been books upon books about project management and how to effectively ensure that large undertakings or events of extraordinary magnitude run smoothly.

Yet, within the book of Nehemiah we discover an individual who together with the wider community rebuilt the wall of a large city in 52 days. This book must therefore provide us with an insight into project management from the greatest Project Manager in all eternity.

Nehemiah's journey begins when he has growing concern for the city of Jerusalem and its sorry state. Prior to becoming a famous project manager, Nehemiah was living in a lap of luxury as cup bearer to the King of Persia. Whilst content and serving exceedingly well, news reaches him of the state of the exiles in Judah.

Neh 1:1-4

The words of Nehemi'ah the son of Hacali'ah. Now it happened in the month of Chislev, in the twentieth year, as I was in Susa the capital, 2 that Hana'ni, one of my brethren, came with certain men out of Judah; and I asked them concerning the Jews that survived, who had escaped exile, and concerning Jerusalem.

3 And they said to me, "The survivors there in the province who escaped exile are in great trouble and

shame; the wall of Jerusalem is broken down, and its gates are destroyed by fire."

4 When I heard these words I sat down and wept, and mourned for days; and I continued fasting and praying before the God of heaven. RSV

The news he received concerning Jerusalem was disconcerting for Nehemiah and led him into a state of mourning and repentance.

For days Nehemiah fasted and prayed before God and sought favour and success in his bid to serve in the restoration and reformation of Jerusalem. Simply put Nehemiah cared enough to seek the Lord and enquire about Jerusalem.

Considering his position and influence as cupbearer to the king (which was a very influential position) he was under no obligation to even think about Jerusalem and the state it was in. Yet, Nehemiah reveals something important about God ideas. For God to work through someone it is necessary for that individual to have concern and compassion for someone else's affliction and hardship.

Neh 1:5-11

5 And I said, "O Lord God of heaven, the great and terrible God who keeps covenant and steadfast love with those who love him and keep his commandments; 6 let thy ear be attentive, and thy eyes open, to hear the prayer of thy servant which I now pray before thee day and night for the people of Israel thy servants,

confessing the sins of the people of Israel, which we have sinned against thee. Yea, I and my father's house have sinned.

7 We have acted very corruptly against thee, and have not kept the commandments, the statutes, and the ordinances which thou didst command thy servant Moses. RSV

Furthermore, Nehemiah proceeds to remind God of the instruction He gave Moses concerning the people of Israel; how the fate and restoration of people of Israel was dependent on the state of their hearts and their obedience.

> **Key**
>
> Learn to keep a God idea a secret until the appointed time to impart the vision.

8 Remember the word which thou didst command thy servant Moses, saying, 'If you are unfaithful, I will scatter you among the peoples; 9 but if you return to me and keep my commandments and do them, though your dispersed be under the farthest skies, I will gather them thence and bring them to the place which I have chosen, to make my name dwell there.'

It was important for Nehemiah to not only recognize the state of Israel but to remind God of His word and commitment to His people.

10 They are thy servants and thy people, whom thou hast redeemed by thy great power and by thy strong hand. 11 O Lord, let thy ear be attentive to the prayer of thy servant, and to the prayer of thy servants who

43

delight to fear thy name; and give success to thy servant today, and grant him mercy in the sight of this man."RSV

In the verses to follow, we see that Nehemiah's prayer was answered and he found favour with the king and was released to attend to matters to do with the reconstruction of Jerusalem's wall and city gate. Moreover, Nehemiah was able to ask the king for safe passage and access to resources to ensure the success of his trip and the work at hand.

Neh 2:11-13

11 So I came to Jerusalem and was there three days. 12 Then I arose in the night, I and a few men with me; and I told no one what my God had put into my heart to do for Jerusalem. There was no beast with me but the beast on which I rode. RSV

What is clear from the text is that God had given Nehemiah a task in Jerusalem. As he surveyed the city at night he kept what God had told him to do in his heart. Nehemiah kept and guarded jealously the idea that God had given him ensuring that he would only reveal it at the appointed time.

Like a good project manager Nehemiah analyzed the work at hand, assessing the walls and gates so as to establish the extent of the challenge at hand and also to develop the necessary response and plan.

Importantly, this was also necessary to keep from drawing unnecessary attention from Israel's enemies namely Sanballat and Tobiah. Finally, having seen the state of the city of God, Nehemiah made his rallying cry to the leaders of the city.

Neh 2:17-18

17 Then I said to them, "You see the trouble we are in, how Jerusalem lies in ruins with its gates burned. Come, let us build the wall of Jerusalem, that we may no longer suffer disgrace." 18 And I told them of the hand of my God which had been upon me for good, and also of the words which the king had spoken to me. And they said, "Let us rise up and build." So they strengthened their hands for the good work.RSV

It was imperative for Nehemiah to present the reality of Jerusalem's situation without leaving the people in total despair. His challenge to the people was not merely a motivation to restore or rebuild the walls but also to remove and do away with the disgrace and shame that was upon the people.

Nehemiah went on further to make clear the favour that had been extended to him by God his project sponsor and by King Artaxerxes.

The rousing cry from the people was clear and Nehemiah a cup bearer to the king was able to rally a whole city to rebuild the city walls and gates. Nehemiah's story is amazing because he was able to bring together people from all walks of life to participate in the work of rebuilding and restoring the city.

Among the labourers were priests, jewelers, perfumer-makers, goldsmiths and even rulers of certain sections of the city. (Nehemiah 3 RSV)

What's more, amid resistance from neighbouring tribes this team of diverse builders continued to skillfully and tirelessly build the wall with one heart and objective, to restore the city. In the midst of construction and external pressure from Jerusalem's enemies Nehemiah continued to seek God's will and support.

Neh 4:4-6

4 Hear, O our God, for we are despised; turn back their taunt upon their own heads, and give them up to be plundered in a land where they are captives. 5 Do not cover their guilt, and let not their sin be blotted out from thy sight; for they have provoked thee to anger before the builders.

In the face of opposition and a disenfranchised people, low on motivation and drive, Nehemiah was able to stir up passion and desire.

6 So we built the wall; and all the wall was joined together to half its height. For the people had a mind to work. RSV

As the restoration of the city's walls and gates was continuing, something more significant was happening; reformation was taking place in the hearts of the people, including their nobles and leaders.

Socially and morally the city of Jerusalem was in just as sorry a state as the walls and the gates. Leaders were abusing their subjects and the little resources available for sustenance were deferred as tax to the king.

Nehemiah went about setting a standard of honour and integrity within the city among the leaders and people. It wasn't just the physical constructs of the city that needed restoration but the hearts and characters of the people.

Neh 6:15-16

> So the wall was finished on the twenty-fifth day of the month Elul, in fifty-two days. 16 And when all our enemies heard of it, all the nations round about us were afraid and fell greatly in their own esteem; for they perceived that this work had been accomplished with the help of our God. RSV

What may have been a challenging and insurmountable task considering the sheer magnitude of the project at hand was fulfilled in record time and achieved more than just restoration of Jerusalem's city wall and gates.

Firstly, there was a sense of unity and dignity among all the people of the city. Secondly, social and economic interaction among the people was restored and everybody was dealing fairly with one another not exacting usury (exorbitant interest charges).

Furthermore, worship was reinstituted in the city as people not only celebrated their success but celebrated the fact that God was among them and had worked through them.

Ultimately, the surrounding tribes and nations saw the influence of God through a downtrodden people working together to build the city walls in 52 days.

So through Nehemiah we know that God ideas can be large projects or initiatives that affect the fate and state of a city and a nation.

Solomon – the architect and philosopher

2 Chron 1:1-3

> 1 Solomon the son of David established himself in his kingdom, and the Lord his God was with him and made him exceedingly great. 2 Solomon spoke to all Israel, to the commanders of thousands and of hundreds, to the judges, and to all the leaders in all Israel, the heads of fathers' houses. RSV

Key to the Roman Empire's militaristic foreign policy, were maxims written by military writers such as Vegetius like, "He who desires peace must prepare for war." (Hadas 1965 pg 89)

> Key
> God ideas can reflect the wisdom of God in different disciplines.

Yet, what we discover with Solomon was that peace in his kingdom was not built on the basis of preemptive conquests of surrounding kingdoms but, on the basis of the wisdom he received from God. Also it was in the fact that the Lord was with him and made him exceedingly great.

2 Chron 1:7-12

> 7 In that night God appeared to Solomon, and said to him, "Ask what I shall give you." 8 And Solomon said to God, "Thou hast shown great and steadfast love to David my father, and hast made me king in his stead. 9 O Lord God, let thy promise to David my father be now fulfilled, for thou hast made me king over a people as many as the dust of the earth. 10 Give me now wisdom

and knowledge to go out and come in before this people, for who can rule this thy people, that is so great?"

11 God answered Solomon, "Because this was in your heart, and you have not asked possessions, wealth, honor, or the life of those who hate you, and have not even asked long life, but have asked wisdom and knowledge for yourself that you may rule my people over whom I have made you king, 12 wisdom and knowledge are granted to you. I will also give you riches, possessions, and honor, such as none of the kings had who were before you, and none after you shall have the like."RSV

Solomon's kingdom was famous because it was a growing and thriving kingdom that had peace with all the surrounding kingdoms. He was reputably wise and this wisdom reflected in the way his nation was run.

Yet, Solomon never used military might to subjugate or enforce peace as according to Vegetius but, he built his kingdom on the wisdom and knowledge he received from God.

Solomon was more than just a great king; he was also an established architect who was credited with building God's temple. To Solomon we also attribute numerous proverbs that still ring true in this modern age.

We can also attribute to Solomon an economic climate of great stability and prosperity. (1 Kings 10:23-27 RSV) Not only was his dwellings furnished with gold but the Bible says that silver was as common as stone in

Jerusalem. Also that choice building tools like cedar wood was as common as the sycamore. He also made Jerusalem a significant centre of commerce importing goods from Egypt and exporting them to the Kings of the Hittites and the Kings of Syria. God's wisdom through Solomon had an effect an the mundane aspects of life and livelihood.

Furthermore, in the book of Ecclesiastes we discover the reflections of a man who had lived his life. His unfettered treatise of the vanity of man captures the futility of life's endeavours outside of God's will and plan. Thus, Solomon having drifted from God concludes his reflections aptly...

Eccl 12:13

> 13 The end of the matter; all has been heard. Fear God, and keep his commandments; for this is the whole duty of man. RSV

From design feats to commerce and trade and perspectives on human endeavor, Solomon stands out as an individual who embraced the God idea. This also led to Solomon discovering and unpacking lots of wisdom and reflection and achieving extraordinary levels of political and economic administration.

> *Importantly, Solomon reveals that God ideas can be diverse, expressing different aspects of human endeavour, from architecture, to philosophy and administration.*

Noah – Boat designer

God Ideas also reflect God's judgement and Noah is an apt story that reveals to us how God brings judgement and redemption to the earth using an innovative boat designer and builder. The ark was an engineering and design feat ahead of its time.

> **Key**
>
> Obeying God's instruction, leads to ideas that make an impact on future generations.

Gen 6:13-22

13 And God said to Noah, "I have determined to make an end of all flesh; for the earth is filled with violence through them; behold, I will destroy them with the earth. 14 Make yourself an ark of gopher wood; make rooms in the ark, and cover it inside and out with pitch.

15 This is how you are to make it: the length of the ark three hundred cubits, its breadth fifty cubits, and its height thirty cubits. 16 Make a roof for the ark, and finish it to a cubit above; and set the door of the ark in its side; make it with lower, second, and third decks.

17 For behold, I will bring a flood of waters upon the earth, to destroy all flesh in which is the breath of life from under heaven; everything that is on the earth shall die. 18 But I will establish my covenant with you; and you shall come into the ark, you, your sons, your wife, and your sons' wives with you. RSV

The ark was a clear display of God's judgment against sin that had overtaken the world. In the instruction God gives to Noah, there is a clear reference to the reason why the ark was to be constructed.

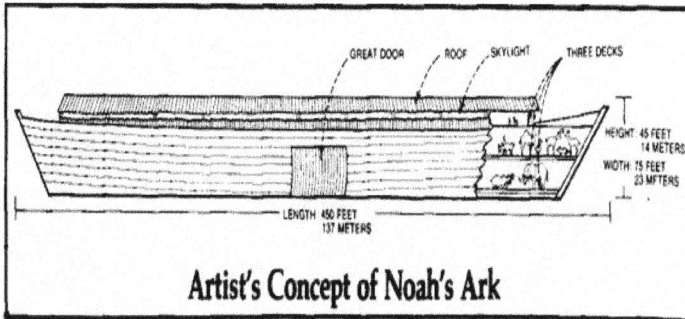

Artist's Concept of Noah's Ark

Figure 3 Noah's Ark SOURCE ©1983, 2004 John Walvoord and Roy Zuck. The Bible Knowledge Commentary: Old Testament published by David C Cook. Publisher permission required to reproduce. All rights reserved.

More than the destruction of the earth, the ark was also an example of God's redemption and plan to restore the earth through Noah.

Though God was about to destroy the earth because of sin, His plan included the redemption of the animals He had created and his most prized possession; man (Noah and his family).

Implicitly, God's instruction to Noah also revealed God's trust in Noah's ability to interpret instructions and reveal them in action.

It may be implied or overly stretched but, there is no explicit reference to the design of the boat that Noah was to build; he was only given measurements. It seemed the design and final outcome of the boat was implicitly left to Noah's interpretation.

But as he went about with his task what may be confirmed through scripture first and foremost, then archeology and history is that Noah built something that could carry all the animals we have today and float for 40 days over rough flood waters.

Whenever God gets involved in creation something innovative will appear that affects the world. Noah accepted and surrendered to God's will and what we can clearly see through the story is that he revealed God's glory and thus brought transformation and redemption to creation and the world. Furthermore, Noah affected boat design and the shipping industry for generations.

"It is well to remember that the architect of Noah's ark was the omniscient scientist whose ways are past finding out though men have learned much from him over the centuries." (Footnote Amplified Bible)

In 1609 at Hoorn in Holland P. Jansen produced a vessel after the pattern of the ark only smaller where he proved it was well adapted to floating and would carry cargo greater than one third than any other form of like cubicle content.

The ark can be credited to have revolutionized shipping. In 1900 every ship on the high seas was definitely inclined toward the proportions of the ark as verified by Lloyd's register of shipping World Almanac. (Footnote Amplified Bible)

> *Evidently, we can conclude that Noah's ark (God's Idea) affected the development of an industry for generations to come. God Ideas will affect the endeavours and enterprise of man.*

Daniel – Astute Politician

Politics is often described as a 'dirty game' and much of what we know in history is that it has been tainted by scandals, deception and trickery which confirm that this is somewhat true. But in Daniel we find a very gifted and astute politician who governs with integrity and justice to the glory of God in the midst of the 'dirt'.

> Key
>
> God ideas affect the politics of men, and government structures of nations.

One of the things we can pick up from the book of Daniel is that he was a man who survived in the political systems and structures of two great kingdoms (Babylon and Medo-Persia) between the years 605BC and 534BC.

The political climate in those days would've carried as much intrigue and trickery as the politics in our modern times. But how was it possible for a foreign exile to ascend to a position second to the King? Additionally, what skills did Daniel have to survive in political office?

Firstly, when an historic king of Babylon, Nebuchadnezzar had a few troubling dreams he called his wise men and magicians to help him interpret the dreams. Knowing that these men had the potential to lie to him he presented them with a life threatening challenge.

He asked them to tell him what he had dreamed and also to provide the interpretation. Certain of death the magicians and wise men begged the king, "There is no man on earth who can meet the king's demand.

Furthermore, no king has ever asked for such a thing. Hence what you are asking for can only be revealed by the gods who do not dwell in the flesh."

Instead of showing mercy the king is angered and goes on further to pass a decree that all the wise men be destroyed. This moment in the history of Babylon poses a great opportunity for the intervention of God.

Instead of providing an opportunity for the wise men to gain prestige and wealth, Daniel was to testify and exalt the name of the Living God to the king of Babylon. It is here that we catch a glimpse of God's omniscience and wisdom at work against the wisdom and ways of man.

When the captain of the king's army arrived to kill Daniel and his friends under authority of the king's decree, Daniel started by dealing discretely and prudently with him. Daniel's intent was to find out why the king wanted him and all the other wise men dead.

When Daniel understood why the king had passed such a harsh decree, he proceeded to beg the king for some time to consider the challenge the king had given. Daniel then went away to seek the Lord and to find an appropriate and accurate response to the king.

In the evening, Daniel received the information he required from the Lord in a vision. He then proceeded to make a bold and powerful confession that revealed the power of God.

Dan 2:19-25

19 Then the mystery was revealed to Daniel in a vision of the night. Then Daniel blessed the God of heaven. 20 Daniel said: RSV

Nothing more is inspiring than to reflect on Daniel's confession of faith as it reveals God's supremacy over the wisdom of man and over rulers and the politics of any given age.

"Blessed be the name of God for ever and ever. to whom belong wisdom and might. 21 He changes times and seasons; he removes kings and sets up kings; he gives wisdom to the wise and knowledge to those who have understanding; 22 he reveals deep and mysterious things; he knows what is in the darkness, and the light dwells with him. 23 To thee, O God of my fathers, I give thanks and praise, for thou hast given me wisdom and strength, and hast now made known to me what we asked of thee, for thou hast made known to us the king's matter." RSV

We also catch a glimpse of Daniel's integrity and respect for life. Instead of seizing this opportunity to eliminate any of his 'political' rivals in the palace, he uses it to save them.

24 Therefore Daniel went in to Ar'i-och, whom the king had appointed to destroy the wise men of Babylon; he went and said thus to him, "Do not destroy the wise men of Babylon; bring me in before the king, and I will show the king the interpretation."

25 Then Ar'i-och brought in Daniel before the king in haste, and said thus to him: "I have found among the exiles from Judah a man who can make known to the king the interpretation." RSV

It is at this moment, that Daniel becomes a significant part of the Babylonian empire within the palace courts serving the politics of the day as a testimony of God's wisdom and power. He is established as the ruler over Babylon and head of all the wise men.

Dan 2:27-30

27 Daniel answered the king, "No wise men, enchanters, magicians, or astrologers can show to the king the mystery which the king has asked, 28 but there is a God in heaven who reveals mysteries, and he has made known to King Nebuchadnez'zar what will be in the latter days. Your dream and the visions of your head as you lay in bed are these: 29 To you, O king, as you lay in bed came thoughts of what would be hereafter, and he who reveals mysteries made known to you what is to be. 30 But as for me, not because of any wisdom that I have more than all the living has this mystery been revealed to me, but in order that the interpretation may be made known to the king, and that you may know the thoughts of your mind. RSV

Daniel goes on to testify to the King of Babylon that there is a God in heaven who is all-knowing and powerful, who has revealed the future to the king in his dream. Daniel proceeds to interpret Nebuchadnezzar's dream.

We catch a glimpse of Daniel's humility and willingness to be used by God to convey what God wants to say to Nebuchadnezzar. He directs and acknowledges the source of the knowledge he dispenses as God the revealer of mysteries.

Surviving the winds of change

Secondly, when Daniel had settled and established himself in the palace and was excelling in service, he came under the rule of a 62 year old Persian king called Darius. It is easy to gloss over these stories

> **Key**
>
> People will recognize and acknowledge an excellent spirit in you.

without taking a lot of cognizance of the apparent and significant changes that were taking place as the incumbent power of Babylon was being overwhelmed by the emerging power of Medo-Persia.

It is in this context that we see more of the excellence of God ideas on the government and politics of the day. With these impending changes in empire came changes in the structure of government.

The new Medo-Persian king Darius decided to set up some government structures of his own which included 120 satraps (princes, protectors of the realm) and 3 presidents. In the process of reshuffling his cabinet, Darius noticed that there was an excellent spirit in Daniel (Dan 6: 3b RSV) and decided to make Daniel the head of the 3 presidents and 120 satraps. In doing this Darius made Daniel the head of the whole kingdom second only to him.

Naturally, this didn't go down well with other presidents and the satraps and so they connived to bring down Daniel and tarnish his name.

When all their attempts to discredit Daniel came to no effect because Daniel was faithful and no error could be found in him, these men then hatched another plan..."We shall not find any reason for complaint against Daniel unless it is connection with the law of His God." (Dan 6:5 RSV)

They all went together to the king...

Dan 6:6-9

6 Then these presidents and satraps came [tumultuously] together to the king and said to him, King Darius, live forever! 7 All the presidents of the kingdom, the deputies and the satraps, the counselors and the governors, have consulted and agreed that the king should establish a royal statute and make a firm decree that whoever shall ask a petition of any god or man for thirty days, except of you, O king, shall be cast

into the den of lions. 8 Now, O king, establish the decree and sign the writing that it may not be changed, according to the law of the Medes and Persians, which cannot be altered. 9 So King Darius signed the writing and the decree. AMP

Instead of bowing to the pressure and decree that had been signed by the king, Daniel continued to do what he had previously done; he prayed and gave thanks to God 3 times a day. Daniel knew who the true authority of all kingdoms was. When the satraps and presidents saw that Daniel was still praying they went to the king and reminded him of the royal decree...

Dan 6:12-14

12 Then they came near and said before the king concerning his prohibitory decree, Have you not signed an edict that any man who shall make a petition to any god or man within thirty days, except of you, O king, shall be cast into the den of lions? The king answered and said, The thing is true, according to the law of the Medes and Persians, which cannot be changed or repealed. 13 Then they said before the king, That Daniel, who is one of the exiles from Judah, does not regard or pay any attention to you, O king, or to the decree that you have signed, but makes his petition three times a day. 14 Then the king, when he heard these words, was much distressed [over what he had done] and set his mind on Daniel to deliver him; and he labored until the sun went down to rescue him. AMP

But the conspirators did not relent and continued to badger the king until he gave in and instructed that Daniel be thrown into the lion's den.

It is amazing in verse 14 to see how much of an impact and influence Daniel had as an exile in the politics of a nation.

Firstly, that there were men who conspired against him to remove from his post but most importantly, Daniel's influence on the king. Not only was the king (often a demigod) repentant but he was also resolute to save one of his most influential and effective civil servants Daniel from his erroneous decree.

Having labored until the sun set and failed, the king made a bold and profound proclamation, which clearly reflects the impact and influence Daniel had on Darius.

Dan 6:16

> The king said to Daniel, May your God, whom you are serving continually, deliver you! AMP

Darius recognized Daniel's devotion to God and in one sentence prayed for Daniel's deliverance. Inevitably, Daniel then spent the night locked up in a den full of hungry and ravenous lions. In the meantime, the king fasted and spent the night without any entertainment or sleep. It is amazing to see how Daniel's unflinching devotion to God brought the king of the most powerful nation of the age to humble submission and surrender.

When morning came the king hurried to the lion's den brimming with faith and expectation. He called out to

Daniel, "Servant of the living God has the God you continually serve saved you from the lions?"

This reflects something that was happening in the king's heart all through the night. Darius was desirous to see the hand of the Lord at work to save Daniel.

Daniel's reverence of God and courage in harsh and very difficult political situations reveals how God ideas affect political systems.

When individuals continue to stand for and trust in God, it is possible for God's glory to be seen miraculously so that a pompous and overly worshiped king forsakes all his honour and hurries down to the den of lions to see the salvation of the Lord.

Instead of the king going on to say, "Well done Daniel for surviving and staving off the lions' attacks throughout the night." He makes an amazing statement of faith to all nations, people and languages,

Dan 6:25-28

May peace be multiplied to you! 26 I make a decree that in all my royal dominion men must tremble and fear before the God of Daniel, for He is the living God, enduring and steadfast forever, and His kingdom shall not be destroyed and His dominion shall be even to the end [of the world]. 27 He is a Savior and Deliverer, and He works signs and wonders in the heavens and on the earth — He Who has delivered Daniel from the power of the lions. 28 So this [man] Daniel prospered in the reign of Darius and in the reign of Cyrus the Persian. AMP

Much like the decree that was proposed by Daniel's enemies, this decree made by Darius on behalf of Daniel was to stand as a law in the land. It is amazing to think of a 'secular' nation creating legislature or laws relating to worship and reverence of the God of Heaven. This is in spite of the fact that Persia had its own idols and gods. Darius confidently recognizes the true Saviour and Deliverer of men.

> *This is an amazing proclamation from the leader of a great 'secular' kingdom that reveals the power of a God idea expressed in the politics of the day. We see from this that there are some people with God ideas that engage and influence politics.*

Job - Reflections of a downtrodden and 'accursed' man

For the philosopher (lover of wisdom), in search of wisdom and understanding, Job provides insight into the definition of true wisdom. Job was a man who had endured severe testing and hardship.

> **Key**
>
> True wisdom is found in and with God.

He had lost all his possessions and his family had been wiped out. To add insult to injury his friends instead of bringing him comfort, were questioning his integrity and character. In the midst of trying circumstances and burgeoning frustrations, Job makes a significant discovery.

Job came to understand that in all the pursuits of men, wisdom is a prime quest. In all of man's exploits and adventures (exploration, mining and industry) wisdom cannot be found. More so that,

Job 28:21-22

> It is hidden from the eyes of all living, and knowledge of it is withheld from the birds of the heavens. 22 Abaddon (the place of destruction) and Death say, We have [only] heard the report of it with our ears. AMP

Job came to the conclusion that nothing created in heaven, earth or beneath the earth could be the source of wisdom rather that wisdom could only be found in God.

Job imparts something very profound when he states that wisdom is hidden from all living things including the birds of the heavens that soar to many heights.

But, the most amazing thing he states is that Abaddon and death have only heard a report, other versions say a rumour of it.

So often we are easily deceived by the devil and it may be because we do not fully comprehend the true source of wisdom. Job clearly reveals that there is no creature or part of creation that is in possession of wisdom. Additionally, death and Hades only hear rumours that there is such a thing as wisdom. In his search and reflection, Job comes to a very significant conclusion to his contemplation...

Job 28:23-24

God understands the way [to Wisdom] and He knows the place of it [Wisdom is with God alone]. 24 For He looks to the ends of the earth and sees everything under the heavens. AMP

Essentially, Job a man in difficult circumstances was asking the proverbial, "Why me?" question when he comes to a conclusion that the only source of wisdom is God. Key to this discovery is the truth that God is omniscient (all knowing and all seeing). Job shows us that God ideas can arise out of difficult situations, as powerful and inspirational reflections.

Job 28:28

[28] But to man He said, Behold, the reverential and worshipful fear of the Lord — that is Wisdom; and to depart from evil is understanding. AMP

Nothing is more important to Job than to discover in his circumstances the very essence of wisdom. In all human endeavours we find ourselves asking famous philosophical questions, Job presents a powerful answer to our deep search for wisdom.

Beyond all things we see around us, the beginning of wisdom is when we fear the Lord. Reverence and respect of God's name is the beginning of a practical and transformational approach to life.

A God idea is not merely restricted to spiritual and physical activities but it also affects our thoughts and intellectual perspectives and views. In the midst of trying and upsetting discussions about his character and the state of his affairs, Job reveals to us that God ideas also affect the very roots of our thoughts and opinions about life.

Chapter 3.

The wisdom of God

Through these Old Testament characters we capture a glimpse of the amazing things that God can do when individuals submit to him and do things to His glory. We catch a glimpse of great works of art and craftsmanship, groundbreaking

> **Key**
>
> God's wisdom is revealed in the death and resurrection of Christ Jesus.

economic theory and management, project management 101 in practice, political aptitude and unique and effective military strategy and profound perspectives on life.

In the New Testament I believe there is much more of the same yet in a more profound way, as the manifold wisdom of God works through the church – challenging principalities and powers in heavenly places.

This is because, prior to Christ dying on the Cross, much of what the Old Testament characters experienced was moments of individual inspiration. They didn't have an ever present encounter with the Holy Spirit, thus much of what God did then and was to do in the future, remained unsearchable and wholly mysterious.

Paul on the other hand reveals to us that what the Old Testament characters encountered in part, we now can fully enjoy because the mystery has now been revealed.

As much as Job explored wisdom and came to a powerful conclusion, he didn't fully capture the depth of God's wisdom which Paul says is now revealed through the church. In Daniel's exploits as a prophet of God under the political regime of two empires, he did not fully reveal the power and authority of God over the kings of the earth.

For we know that the great heroes of faith, "...having obtained a good report through faith, received not the promise. God having provided some better thing for us that they without us should not be made perfect." (Hebrews 11:39-40 RSV)

What they believed God for was to be revealed and completed in all those who would believe and rely on the name of Jesus Christ.

Furthermore, God was also going to reveal His wisdom through the church so that the prince of the air and his minions would see the glorious work of redemption throughout creation.

Eph 3:8-11

[8]To me, though I am the very least of all the saints, this grace was given, to preach to the Gentiles the unsearchable riches of Christ, [9] and to make all men see what is the plan of the mystery hidden for ages in God

70

who created all things; 10 that through the church the manifold wisdom of God might now be made known to the principalities and powers in the heavenly places.

11 This was according to the eternal purpose which he has realized in Christ Jesus our Lord, RSV

It is this new work of God that is necessary in our modern day, as it rises out of a new perspective (testament) for human endeavour and achievement.

God's deep intent and wisdom is to reveal the eternal purpose of His nature and will which we know is fulfilled and complete in Christ the Lord of lords.

Figure 4 A new perspective

This wisdom requires that we consider and develop a new perspective on life and how we live it Fig 4 adapted from Hein Van Wyk (2006). We must,

1. Have a vision for the Kingdom of God. That is to say we must have a glimpse and an active goal to see God's rule and reign expressed throughout the earth through the preaching and expression of the gospel of Christ.
2. We must have a clear strategy for compassion and expression of God's love, engaging in practical and transformational social action.
3. Our view of work must be immersed in the Lordship of Christ.
4. Our intellectual leanings and opines must be like Christ's (having the mind of Christ and an intelligible act of worship). (Phil 2: 5 and Rom 12:1-3 RSV)
5. We must embrace and lay hold of the ultimate call on our lives as believers, which is to make disciples of all nations.

We must do the right things (the will of God) and do them right (as God has commanded). Thus all we endeavour to do and say must completely align to the wisdom of God.

This new perspective (mindset) and work comes out of the most glorious God Idea, the atoning sacrifice of Jesus that brings salvation and redemption to man. It is when we fix our eyes on Christ like flint, that we will see the gospel reach the ends of the earth. We will see the Gospel transforming dead cultures to living expressions of God's manifold wisdom.

Chapter 4.

'Bara' newness coming through the new man

What is Bara?

Bara newness reflects a position of faith that declares that God is the source of all things and is the one and only true Originator. The term 'Bara' means create in Hebrew. The Bible uses this

> **Key**
>
> God's creative power (Bara) is the cornerstone all God Ideas.

term solely in reference to God's creative power. It is also in reference to God's power to shape things from nothing, such as heaven and earth, humanity, time and context and transformational change (heart, mind and life).

Bara reflects God's ability to bring forth a concept or object from what didn't exist before. Nothing can be more exciting than capturing a glimpse of God's 'Bara' at work within the world. Hence, 'Bara' newness in this chapter is in direct reference to the work of Christ on the Cross and the subsequent salvation of humankind. In speaking about ideas we can ill afford to avoid thought on creativity and the act of creation as represented by God through the Cross of Christ.

Bara represents the core and essence of creativity and is the cornerstone of God ideas during the Old Testament, during the New Testament age and ultimately the end times age.

It is a profound term that reflects the act of a Sovereign God who is the originator, sustainer and regulator of all things.

2 Cor 5:17

17 Therefore, if any one is in Christ, he is a new creation; the old has passed away, behold, the new has come. RSV

Paul makes this very bold statement, that whoever is in Christ is now a new creation. This means that believers have become active participants in the work of resurrection and restoration that Christ began and completed on the Cross. This is also a bold statement of faith.

Paul is proclaiming that there is a present and very spiritual reality permeating the world as people come to a genuine knowledge of God. The old has gone and the new has come! It's something totally unique and different and there is nothing it can be compared to in the past. Every human being who accepts Jesus as Lord and Savior is a wonderful new expression of the glory and majesty of God.

Eph 4:22-24

Strip yourselves of your former nature [put off and discard your old unrenewed self] which characterized your previous manner of life and becomes corrupt through lusts and desires that spring from delusion; 23 And be constantly renewed in the spirit of your mind [having a fresh mental and spiritual attitude],

24 And put on the new nature (the regenerate self) created in God's image, [Godlike] in true righteousness and holiness. AMP

The new man in Christ –

Believers are totally unique in many respects as expressed in Paul's letter to the Ephesians. The new man is an expression of God's will at various levels of human endeavour and enterprise. Unlike the former old self that is characterized by lusts and desires, the new man is renewed in spiritual outlook and mental attitudes and perspectives. The new man is a much clearer reflection of God's image displaying freedom, right standing and holiness.

Christ's work of atonement and reconciliation, as He is called the second Adam (1Cor 15:45- 49 RSV) and His work in restoring us to the image of God, carries so much value and wealth to a world in dire need of answers and direction. Through His creative power, God has taken what was once dead and made a living, vibrant and glorious new man with capacity once more to effectively impact a corrupted earth with His power and glory.

75

Believers represent the initial work of God in His bid to transform all that He has created into an eternal and priceless wonder.

We know this because creation is groaning for the manifestation of the sons of God - when we see the glorious picture of the kingdom of God on earth as it is in heaven (A new heaven and new earth) creation will also be restored and reflect once more the perfect and resplendent beauty of God.

Rom 8:18-24

18 I consider that the sufferings of this present time are not worth comparing with the glory that is to be revealed to us. 19 For the creation waits with eager longing for the revealing of the sons of God; 20 for the creation was subjected to futility, not of its own will but by the will of him who subjected it in hope; 21 because the creation itself will be set free from its bondage to decay and obtain the glorious liberty of the children of God. 22 We know that the whole creation has been groaning in travail together until now; 23 and not only the creation, but we ourselves, who have the first fruits of the Spirit, groan inwardly as we wait for adoption as sons, the redemption of our bodies. RSV

As believers we have become new creatures in Christ. This implies something more than just being able to go to church on a Sunday. Once, before salvation, man was generally subjected to death, but through Christ there is now new life.

Though the new life will be fully revealed when Christ returns a second time when believers are glorified, it is already at work in everyone who believes that Jesus Christ is Lord.

It is this new work that brings about the God idea in modern times post the cross. When every believer surrenders to the will of God, the newness thriving within furnishes us with the tools (ideas) to bring about transformation and revival to the world around us.

The Cross in some respects is similar to the seven days of creation in that Christ has created something new out of nothing. At the very heart of the Cross is the new man equipped with the power and strength to bring transformation. Ultimately, Christ through the new man seeks to make everything new (reference again to Revelation and new heaven and new earth).

Hence, Christ is establishing a new promise to man and the rest of creation. As believers receive Christ as Lord and eagerly seek to fulfill and obey His will, they become agents of this new creation.

We become agents of the 'bara' newness (God's creative ability) that is now indwelling in our hearts and spirits. Our role as believers becomes principal in presenting God's will for people and the world that we live in.

The God idea becomes the function or service we offer as believers to the world in a bid to reveal and display

God's glory and ability to be involved in the matters of man and the rest of creation.

Matt 5: 16

[16]Let your light so shine before men that they may see your good works and give glory to your Father in heaven. RSV

It is also important in fulfilling God's redemptive plan which seeks not to totally obliterate creation but to establish a new heaven and new earth, no longer corrupted by sin.

Imagine bringing Bara newness to all aspects of human life. Not merely purporting moral perspectives but, believers influencing and working to shape the very roots of human culture in every area.

Recognizing Bara Newness (Dorothy L. Sayer)

According to Dorothy Sayer a theologian there are 5 things that can help us see and recognize Bara newness at work in our lives and communities,

1. Bara newness is unprecedented (Isa. 43:15-21 RSV)-- the first of its kind, that which did not exist before, that which is irreducible to something known, the unheard of.

Instantly, what comes to mind is when Paul says that we are a new creation (something inimitable designed and expressed)

2. Bara newness is humanly unforeseeable (Num. 16:30). It has the quality of surprise, of hiddenness brought to light--the quality of the unexpected and

unpredictable. God's redemptive work in man is even a wonder to the angels. (1 Peter 1:12 RSV)

3. Bara newness is valuable (Gen 29: Isa 41:17-20 RSV). It cannot be novelty for novelty's sake. It must solve a problem, serve a function, and be workable, yet beautiful, fitting, elegant.

4. Bara newness is transformational in that it can become part of tradition and undergo transformation, re-creation (Gal. 6:15; Eph. 2:15 RSV).

5. Bara newness is lasting. It does not lose its lustre after repeated examination and contemplation. This is a newness that never perishes.

These are key points to help us in pursuit of our work and endeavours. They also give us the ability to recognize when we are onto something eternally significant, the **God Idea** that brings about lasting transformation in communities. It will be coming out of the work of the Spirit indwelling in us.

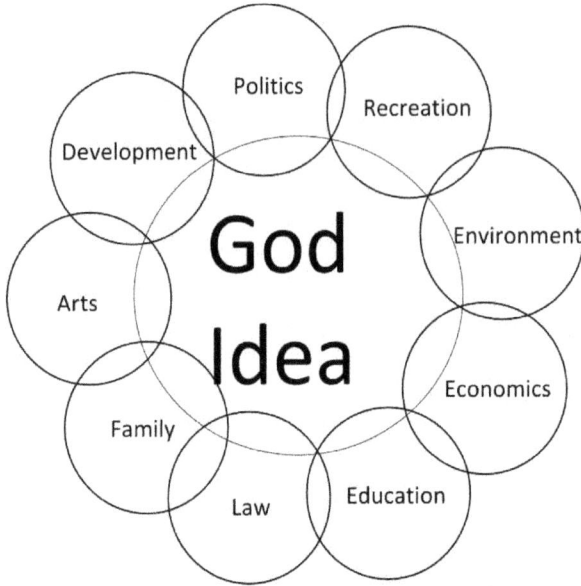

Figure 5 God Ideas spreading - *in practice*

When believers surrender to God's will and pursue the God idea within, they'll be people who will govern with integrity and honesty. Children and students will grow in wisdom, knowledge and inspiration to serve the King of kings and their fellow man.

We will see economies built on the foundation of stewardship and responsibility. In our pursuit for human dignity we will foster love through the ideals of human responsibility over human rights as everybody seeks to serve others above their own greedy ambitions and ends.

Importantly, our exploits will not diminish or negate the superiority and preeminence of God's creative ability but reflect or image this attribute of God. Arthur Koestler says something profound,

"The creative act is not an act of creation in the sense of the Old Testament [Genesis 1]. It does not create something out of nothing it uncovers selects, reshuffles, combines synthesizes already existing facts ideas, faculties skills. The more familiar the parts, the more striking the new whole." (Koestler 1964 The Act of creation)

In our attempts to capture the 'Bara' in our day to day lives, it is in the different sectors of existence that we uncover, select or synthesize the elements and treasure God has stored in His creation.

Our glory as (Proverbs 25:2 RSV) states is in a fresh and dynamic bid to search out, discover and display the glory of God hidden in Him. Our glory will also be to reveal the boundless treasures hidden in jars of clay as Paul says in (2 Cor 4:7RSV).

Bara newness is an attempt to fully appreciate God's creative power. It also proceeds to present to us the outworking of God's infinite wisdom as displayed to the angelic rulers and authorities through the church.

Chapter 5.

Manifold wisdom in the church

Earlier (Chapter 3) I made mention of the manifold wisdom of God. It is important for us to appreciate God's wisdom that was concealed in past ages that is now clearly

> **Key**
>
> God is actively involved in His creation, especially man.

reflected and represented in Christ Jesus.

Eph 3:9-10

> 9 Also to enlighten all men and make plain to them what is the plan [regarding the Gentiles and providing for the salvation of all men] of the mystery kept hidden through the ages and concealed until now in [the mind of] God Who created all things by Christ Jesus. 10 [The purpose is] that through the church the complicated, many-sided wisdom of God in all its infinite variety and innumerable aspects might now be made known to the angelic rulers and authorities (principalities and powers) in the heavenly sphere. AMP

This passage reveals a few things about God's wisdom firstly, that it is manifold meaning that it is diverse having many different forms and aspects like a resplendent crystal. Secondly, that it is displayed through the church. Lastly, that it is directed towards the dark rulers of this age. What are the things that can be displayed as Godly wisdom through the church? It is true that we are not of this world and it is also true that we are in this world.

So we may ask further before even answering the first question that, what does the world see of our inherited nature as believers?

It is here that we discover the inherent and unstoppable power of God's kingdom as it has been established through and by the Cross of Jesus Christ. Importantly, God's wisdom isn't limited to how we spend our days in church on a Sunday or Wednesday (midweek meeting).

It is important to understand that God's wisdom is diverse and effectively permeates every aspect of creation. God is not limited in His involvement with His creation. It is imperative therefore, that believers appreciate that God is engaged in creation in two ways.

He is transcendent, that means that He exists outside of creation as an independent entity that is fully self contained and sustaining. In being transcendent God reflects his supremacy over creation as its Originator and designer.

He is also immanent, meaning that He also exists and indwells within His creation. This is also refers to his dynamic and constant involvement in creation. Another way of considering immanence is to simply say that he remains involved and He did not pull away once He had finished creating.

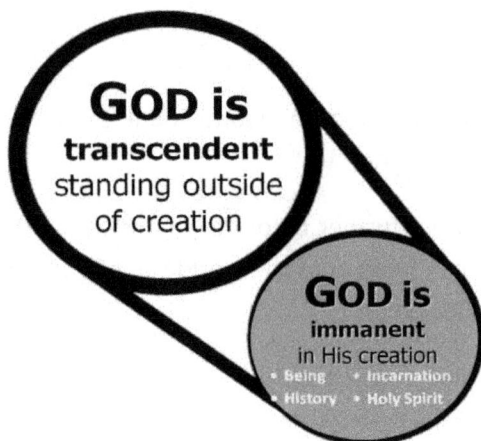

Figure 6 God's *Involvement* in Creation Source Hein Van Wyk
Biblical Worldview seminar

Rom 1:20

[20] For ever since the creation of the world His invisible
nature and attributes, that is, His eternal power and
divinity, have been made intelligible and clearly
discernible in and through the things that have been
made (His handiworks). So [men] are without excuse
[altogether without any defense or justification], [Ps
19:1-4.] AMP

(Romans 1:20 RSV) reveals to us that creation displays
God's invisible attributes so that no man has excuse. So
trees, oceans, animals and all that we see displays and
cries out some of God's attributes and reflects his
eternal power and divinity.

But, the most glorious expression of God's immanence
is when He is revealed through his people. Through
people, God is intent on displaying his wisdom to the
angelic authorities in the heavens through the church.

Peter in (1 Peter 2:12 RSV) makes references to the truth that, what God is doing in his people (believers) is something so amazing that angels who spend their time worshiping God, long to look into this great wonder and mystery.

What mystery is displayed? The angels see a people who were once destined for destruction now carrying a living hope and dedication to God. They also see people ready to live differently and display the light of the Creator to the rest of the world. For believers this is achieved through preaching the gospel but also through our lifestyles and attitude towards God, other people, creation itself and history/or the future (pending history).

Towards God

God's manifold wisdom concerning his character and nature is displayed through the church, as and when we worship Him and display His value and worth. What we reveal to the principalities and rulers in heavenly places is that it is possible for someone who was once destined for destruction to enter boldly into the throne room of God because of the person and nature of Jesus Christ.

When we worship and place great worth on Jesus Christ and what He did for us on the Cross, it provides a glimpse of the depth of God's love and compassion.

Matt 22:37

"And You shall love the Lord your God with all your heart and with all your soul and with all your mind. " RSV

God's wisdom is also displayed through the church when the church acknowledges His attributes like omnipresence (He is everywhere), omniscience (He is all knowing) and omnipotence (He is all powerful).

It is important then for believer's to express this to principalities, that God is in all things, God knows everything (nothing is hidden from him) and that God is all powerful and superior to all other things.

Towards Other People

Matt 22:39

"You shall love your neighbor as yourself." RSV

God's manifold wisdom is also displayed in the way we treat other people. Christ talks about loving our enemies and blessing those who curse us. In a fallen world, there is so much animosity and bad blood between people. We are constantly reminded of this by the media with news of murders, crimes against humanity and the effect of the politics of our day; as manifested in different wars.

Yet, in this seemingly insurmountable depravity, we hear Jesus telling us to love those who curse us (Matt 5:44 RSV).

God's wisdom is expressed to the principalities when we are able to express and serve other people in love. At the heart of the Gospel is the restoration of human dignity; such that it reflects what it was supposed to as the image of God.

When believers desire to express and also to see somebody else (an unbeliever or wicked person) express themselves as the image of God, we will see God's manifold wisdom in human relationships. *"Bind up the broken heart, preach the good news and release from darkness those in prison..."* (Isa 61:1 RSV)

In creation

Creation that is nature, our surroundings, the earth and the universe since man's sin; have seen corruption. The acts of Adam and Eve affected nature and we have a clearer glimpse of the effects of sin in this modern age.

The world as we know it is in constant turmoil and we hear news from all over the world of earthquakes, famines, disease and other forms of destruction. We in this modern age are seeing unprecedented acts of destruction also caused by human greed for success and money. Deforestation and pollution are direct results of our insatiable need for new trends and ideas.

Unapologetically, we warrant the destruction of creation in the interest of a new television or for a bigger and 'better' car or for obscene amounts of money that we will never consume for generations.

How do we display God's wisdom in creation? Once when God created the world, He said that it was good. The principalities and rulers in the heavenly places must once more see that what God made was and is good.

The work of Christ on the cross also involved restoration of what was once man's responsibility before the fall, which is to be stewards of the earth. When Genesis makes reference to man's authority to subdue the earth and have dominion over it, it isn't saying we can go about and do to the earth as we wish.

Gen 1:28

28 And God blessed them and said to them, Be fruitful, multiply, and fill the earth, and subdue it [using all its vast resources in the service of God and man]; and have dominion over the fish of the sea, the birds of the air, and over every living creature that moves upon the earth. AMP

Rather, it is encouraging us to consider and wisely make use of the available resources and to appreciate this earth in the same way that God considers it as good. Subjugation in Genesis is referring to God giving us the power to cultivate and develop the earth and grow things.

As believers we can once more display the manifold wisdom of God in the way we use resources and manage things to the glory of Jesus Christ.

As much as we look back and consider the past as history we must also have a perspective that at some point the future itself will one day also be history. In essence, human beings are living in a time capsule and past, present and future are all intertwined and contribute to what one day may be termed human history.

The question is how we look at time. Peter in (1 Peter 1:24-25 RSV) says this, "All flesh is like the grass and the glory of man is like the flower of the grass. The grass withers and the flower fades away but the word of the Lord endures forever." As human beings we live for a limited and very small period of time in context to God and eternity.

Nevertheless, it is in this mortal frame that we have the opportunity to make an impact on eternity. Our time on earth may be dedicated to our flesh and the glories thereof or it may be dedicated to the Word of God (1Cor 15: 47-50 RSV).

When the church expresses or displays the manifold wisdom of God it has an effect on various aspects of society and creation. The church is inspired to have a godly and wise response to the crises of our time.

Whether it is to pronounce the judgements of God as referred to in Revelation and Matthew 24, in standing for the dignity and rights of the poor and oppressed. Or when providing direction to politicians, by giving them the right perspective of their responsibility to God (no human being has absolute power over another).

Moreover, believers have the express opportunity to draw from God an understanding of all created things and how to make use of them to improve human life (the cure for HIV/AIDS is hidden in nature and known fully by God).

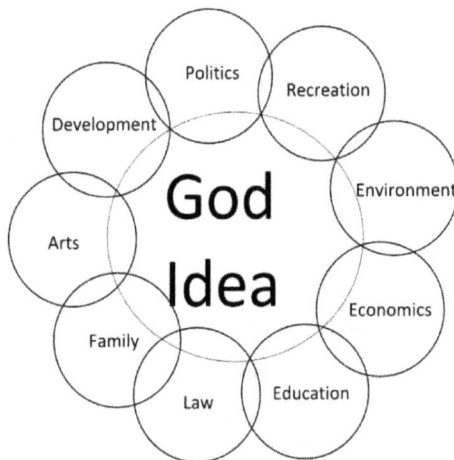

Figure 7 God Ideas spreading - *Manifest through the church*

Ultimately, the manifold wisdom of God expressed through the church is reflected in the mind of Christ. The church that is, every believer is challenged not to lord it over anybody or anything but rather like Christ to take up the attitude of a servant. True wisdom will be reflected by the church when we look to serve. Hence, critical to the expression or manifestation of a God idea is the state of our minds.

Chapter 6.

Renewing of the mind - immanent

Rom 12:1-2

¹ I APPEAL to you therefore, brethren, and beg of you in view of [all] the mercies of God, to make a decisive dedication of your bodies [presenting all your members and faculties] as a living sacrifice, holy (devoted, consecrated) and well pleasing to God, which is your reasonable (rational, intelligent) service and spiritual worship.

> **Key**
>
> **The Word of God renews our thinking and logic.**

² Do not be conformed to this world (this age), [fashioned after and adapted to its external, superficial customs], but be transformed (changed) by the [entire] renewal of your mind [by its new ideals and its new attitude], so that you may prove [for yourselves] what is the good and acceptable and perfect will of God, even the thing which is good and acceptable and perfect [in His sight for you]. AMP

As stated in chapter 4 we have become agents of God's will and 'bara' newness because we have accepted Jesus Christ as our Lord and Saviour. Yet, we often find that there's still a raging battle in and for our minds. As believers we are often the victims and culprits of wrong thinking and ultimately wrong actions. We live our lives in abject confusion and frustration because we have no clear understanding of the new capacity and ability we possess to bring about transformation and revival.

The first verses of Romans 12 present to us the opening practical steps towards releasing a God idea that affects society with the glory of God.

It begins with Paul imploring that believers intently consider the mercy God has provided through salvation by presenting their bodies as living sacrifices. There seems to be a paradox in what Paul is asking believers to do, as in normal terms a sacrifice dies.

But it is once more a glorious glimpse of the work of the Cross in that, "Whoever loses his life for my sake will find it." (Matt 10:39b) In Jesus we are alive and thus Paul can only ask for a living sacrifice that will not perish but have everlasting life to offer up in total service to Christ.

Paul calls this a reasonable and intelligent act of worship. Beyond the songs we sing on Sunday as worship and praise, worship is the act of surrender of all that we are to God. When we surrender to Him it truly reflects worship and total obeisance to the King of kings and his purposes.

For Paul, worship is an act that not only combines faith but also reason and logic. In his request to make or consider something, lie the ingredients of thoughtful consideration, based importantly on the faith we have received. What's more, Paul asks believers to clearly consider the implications and consequence of a decision to totally submit to Jesus.

His next request is that believers avoid conforming to the patterns and thinking of the world but that they be transformed by the renewing of their minds. Paul's reference here to transformation is similar to the word rendering for transfiguration in (Matt 17 RSV) which is *metamorphosis* (a change in look, structure and characteristics). Paul is really challenging believers to consider the biggest and most significant shift in paradigm in the world today.

It isn't from one theoretical framework to the next, but it is a total change in the roots of ideas and thought in general. It is such a shift that will result in a God idea. When believers consider the work of Christ on the Cross and the evident mercy of God and present themselves as living sacrifices whose minds are transformed.

What will be clear is the distinction between the thinking and action of believers and the rest of civilization. The endeavour of a believer will be to hold fast to the teaching of the gospels, and earnest steps towards affecting all aspects of society with new God given perspectives and ideas.

The mind of Christ

Phil 2:5-9

[5]Let this same attitude and purpose and [humble] mind be in you which was in Christ Jesus: [Let Him be your example in humility:]

[6] Who, although being essentially one with God and in the form of God [possessing the fullness of the attributes which make God God], did not think this equality with God was a thing to be eagerly grasped or retained,

[7] But stripped Himself [of all privileges and rightful dignity], so as to assume the guise of a servant (slave), in that He became like men and was born a human being.

[8] And after He had appeared in human form, He abased and humbled Himself [still further] and carried His obedience to the extreme of death, even the death of the cross! [9] Therefore [because He stooped so low] God has highly exalted Him and has freely bestowed on Him the name that is above every name, AMP

This passage challenges us to consider and embrace that same attitude and **humble** mind that was in Christ.

Essentially, it helps us appreciate meekness and the power of servitude. It is case and point that though Christ deserved and was totally worthy to receive the dignity and honour of God, He instead chose to embrace the status of a servant or more explicitly a slave.

Becoming human, Jesus sought not to glorify himself but rather as He so rightly states,

Matt 20:28

28 even as the Son of man came not to be served but to serve, and to give his life as a ransom for many." RSV

For us, this is revolutionary and exemplary thinking, in that though Jesus deserved honour, glory and the privilege of a glorious king; He forsook these privileges in service to all mankind. The zenith of His commitment and obedience to his call to service was His gruesome death on the cross.

Much of our lives are spent in a quest to attain glory, fame and significance. Often all we do is geared towards our comfort and the gratification of self. God ideas are designed to glorify God, whilst meeting the needs of other people. Yet, they don't leave the individual debased and disappointed. Rather, God Ideas also benefit the individual living for and applying a God idea.

As with the example of Christ we see that because He chose to serve, God exalted him and freely bestowed upon him the name that is above every other name. For believers this means that if we follow Christ's example, our greatness will not come as we ambitiously pursue money, power and respect but, when we seek to humbly serve people as exemplified by Jesus.

Believers are graced with such a wonderful opportunity to make a difference and to display the wonder and glory of the name of Jesus, the name that is above every other name. It is when we choose to think differently and apply ourselves doing whatever is...

Whatever is...?

If at all we are to fully enjoy the fruit of a God idea we must prepare to take up new perspectives and thought patterns. God ideas are born out of a mind geared towards servitude and ultimately a deep

> **Key**
>
> The saving grace is a practical tool for transformation.

and well thought out desire to serve and glorify God. Our thoughts must skew so significantly towards a place of profound reflection on whatever is...

Phil 4:8

For the rest, brethren, whatever is true, whatever is worthy of reverence and is honorable and seemly, whatever is just, whatever is pure, whatever is lovely and lovable, whatever is kind and winsome and gracious, if there is any virtue and excellence, if there is anything worthy of praise, think on and weigh and take account of these things [fix your minds on them]. AMP

To truly appreciate and experience a God Idea we must consider that it must glorify God and direct all praise and worship to Him as the author and finisher of our faith.

A God Idea will emerge out of believers as we process and think through the 9 things Paul presents to us as areas of consideration and contemplation in our pursuit of different activities in our society.

1. **True** – *human need for salvation. Our thoughts and the actions resulting thereof must be drawn and inspired by the inalienable truth of God.*
2. **Worthy of reverence** – *God's unlimited and overwhelming power. We must consider and accept that God is the only one deserving reverence and worship*
3. **Honourable and seemly** - *God has all the honour and glory and is above all good.*
4. **Just** – *equity and concern for the oppressed and underprivileged like widows and orphans. God's desire is to bring the good news to the poor and to bind up the broken hearted.*
5. **Pure** – *The perfect example of purity is the blood of the lamb which is the only atonement for sin.*
6. **Lovely** and **Lovable** – *Appreciating God's creation as it displays his invisible properties.*
7. **Kind** – *beautiful feet that bring the good news*
8. **Virtuous** – *a heart full of compassion*
9. **Worthy of praise** – *true servitude and humility*

To think on these things, consider and practice them is imperative. If we can once more look at the world with these lenses, we will be struck by the wonder of God and all He has done.

Once more, the rose bloom will be full of beauty; the graceful motion of a ballet dancer will radiate the beauty of our imaging in God's likeness. We will be struck by the hues of a sunset and the splendor of the skies at night when we look at the billions of stars doted across a vast black canvas. We will see God's economy interact with our businesses, families and industries.

But more importantly we will see that beyond the common grace that God has granted to all creation for continued life (Gen 8: 21-22 RSV), the world is in desperate need for saving grace. Believers will realize that there is a growing need within society for the unmerited favour of God to bring about redemption, salvation and relevant God ideas. As believers take up new perspectives in conformity to Christ they will essentially become ambassadors.

Chapter 7.

Ambassadors of Christ – a vision for the kingdom of God

I am sending you as God to pharaoh

Ex 7:1-2

> 1 THE LORD said to Moses, Behold, I make you as God to Pharaoh [to declare My will and purpose to him]; and Aaron your brother shall be your prophet. AMP

> **Key**
>
> We are unique representatives of God's intentions on earth.

This verse is a very profound passage that reveals the significance of God's involvement in the realm of men. It is here that we see an indication of God's impact on a man so as to unleash the God idea.

Moses' encounter with God at the burning bush reveals a man broken and humbled to a point where he believes he will be of ill effect to the work of God. Whatever the consequences of Moses' initial rejection of God's call, his final obedience results in him being sent to Pharaoh as God (appropriately a representative of God) to fulfill God's plan for the nation of Israel.

God ideas are about presenting the will of God to the world and revealing his purposes and intentions. God ideas challenge the human paradigm with the God paradigm. When a God idea is unleashed it exposes the inadequacies of human ideas and the fallacy of human endeavour outside of God.

Prior to this passage it is revealed that this Pharaoh had forgotten what God had done through Joseph. When the world forgets God, they need to be reminded; thus this is the role of a God Idea. A God idea is there to reveal and represent the agenda of God in a community or to a nation.

Consequently, believers in modern times carry much of the same responsibility as we represent the name of Christ and His kingdom wherever we go. Successively through chapters 24, 25 and 26 of Acts we see Paul serving in the capacity of Ambassador of Christ to the kings of the world.

Hence, we can confidently relate to (Exodus 7:1 RSV) by boldly proclaiming that we are ambassadors of Christ.

We are Christ's ambassadors

2 Cor 5:18-20

[18] But all things are from God, Who through Jesus Christ reconciled us to Himself [received us into favor, brought us into harmony with Himself] and gave to us the ministry of reconciliation [that by word and deed we might aim to bring others into harmony with Him].

[19] It was God [personally present] in Christ, reconciling and restoring the world to favor with Himself, not

counting up and holding against [men] their trespasses [but cancelling them], and committing to us the message of reconciliation (of the restoration to favor).

[20] So we are Christ's ambassadors, God making His appeal as it were through us. We [as Christ's personal representatives] beg you for His sake to lay hold of the divine favor [now offered you] and be reconciled to God. AMP

Importantly, when Paul speaks of us as ambassadors of Christ he is saying this, "That it is no longer I who live but Christ who lives in me." (Gal 2:20 RSV)

When Christ lives in us it is imperative that we understand that we are now outposts of God's Kingdom on earth and thus we represent the will of God on the earth. Ambassadors are known for one particular characteristic; they only share the intentions and views of the state they represent and never share their own/personal opinions about an issue. When Paul calls us ambassadors of Christ he really means that we no longer represent our own agendas, fiefdoms or intentions but we now represent and serve the God's agenda on earth.

This means we only present God's intentions on earth. Imagine what God's government would be like on earth? The simple answer to this is to look at ourselves in the mirror and to see God's government involved in the earth. However we see ourselves in the mirror, we get to understand that we are either representing or misrepresenting the kingdom of God.

Our appeal as ambassadors to the world is one of reconciliation. No matter the cost or challenge our efforts in all that we do must reflect the fact that we have peace with God and God is interested in making peace with men before Christ's second coming which is when He makes war with men who have denied him.

William Barclay on his reflections on (Luke 2:25-35 RSV) says this, "It is not so much God who judges a man; a man judges [condemns] himself; and his judgement is his reaction to Jesus Christ. If, when he is confronted with that goodness and loveliness, his heart runs out in answering love he is within the kingdom. If, so when confronted he remains coldly unmoved or actively hostile, he is condemned." Barclay (1973). Also look at (John 3:17-19 RSV)

We not only represent the interest of God on earth or make declarations of the impending war that is to come but we are also chosen for an assignment according to the commission given. Every believer is gifted, talented and endowed with unique ideas that are relevantly tied to their specific purpose and role in the kingdom of God.

Chapter 8.

Christ's new work

Matt 28:19

"Go therefore and make disciples of all nations..." RSV

When Christ commissions us to go out and make disciples, he is making a request to continue to preach the gospel that he taught and lived, "Repent for the kingdom of God is at hand."(Matt 4:17 RSV) Our mission in this world is to present the will of God in

> **Key**
>
> The Gospel is more than just words and works it's God's ability to shape all levels of society.

all its wonder and diversity. It is to challenge the roots of a nation ideally their beliefs and disciplines (discipline and disciple are from the same root word) in a bid to bring about transformation and renewal.

Making disciples involves God's express wisdom and intent for all creation and also the work of His creative power 'bara' to make all things new once more.

The gospel is more than just words and works, it is an active expression of God's ability to shape and influence society at all levels. Much of the world as we know it is built around ideas and beliefs that shape our activities.

So, when we think of culture we must consider that it comes from the word cultivate meaning that whatever we believe is something that we have nurtured over time.

When Christ commissions believers to go and make disciples of all nations, He is challenging believers to go to different tribes and communities and challenge what they've nurtured over the years.

Tim Keller (2010) a pastor of Redeemer Church in America presents something of great importance here when he says this, "Contextualization is the incarnation of the gospel in a new culture. Because each culture has a worldview or 'world story' at its heart, to reach a new culture the gospel must enter, challenge, and re-tell the story of that culture."

The Gospel at its most potent must invade a given culture be it, Shona tradition or Western post modernity and challenge the entrenched ideas therein and re-tell them (redeem them). The work of salvation then goes beyond a moment of conversion towards a process of transformation and renewal.

Inspired by our call to service believers can truly be inspired to look at different aspects of society from science to entertainment and seek to bring about discipleship and transformation by humbly accepting to serve God and reveal the God idea that God has placed within them. Consider Areopagus...

Areopagus – Mars Hill

In (Acts 17 RSV), Paul presents to us something of great importance about the city and the flow and formulation of ideas when he encounters the men of Mars Hill. During their recreation and leisure, the Greeks and foreign visitors of Athens spent their time on Mars Hill looking to hear of new and novel ideas about the world and life. Now on reading this it may have seemed as though this was unimportant to the overall wellbeing of the nation.

Yet, what is highly evident in the text is that whatever was discussed on Mars Hill was of critical importance to the culture of the day. When Paul observed upon arrival in Athens that there were many idols in the city he was roused to preach but was also drawn to wonder where they were emanating from.

Many of the idols would have developed or formed as ideas and notions of the Greek's foremost love for philosophy. The Greeks were renowned for their love of wisdom (*philos-phy)* and so spent their time searching out matters. Upon reflection and rigorous discussion they would come to a position. I would presuppose that every deity reflected an aspect of their discovery and appreciation of the world and its diverse perspectives of life and death. At the very heart of Athenian life, was the quest for ideas that reflected or helped an individual reflect on the meaning of life.

Ideas discussed and formed on Mars Hill would eventually shape the city's worship, scientific endeavour, recreation, business and so forth. Upon hearing Paul preaching about Christ and His resurrection the men of Athens engaged him further, as they recognized that Paul was teaching something new and altogether 'novel' to them. On hearing him speak continuously some disregarded his proposition, whilst others sought to hear more about this Jesus and what Paul meant by resurrection.

It is interesting to note that at this point the men brought him along to Mars Hill for further inquiry and discussion. From this we can clearly establish that Mars Hill was a place where the ideas and views that were shaped would inevitably affect and effect change in the way of life in Athens. A new idol (form) would essentially emerge from the conclusion and scrutiny of an idea.

Upon entering Mars Hill, Paul recognized this and sought not to antagonize the order of the day and the roots of the culture of the city. Instead Paul seized this opportunity to engage the culture of the day at its roots with truth. We may look and frown upon pagan worship and idolatry sometimes without a full appreciation of its roots or source.

And often, when believers antagonize and challenge people's beliefs without fully appreciating the source from which they emanate, we fail to win over people or to garner and maintain an audience with them. For Paul, Christianity wasn't man's conception or invention but he also appreciated that it faced challenges from other ideas.

It is important for us to appreciate that God ideas don't exist in a vacuum and essentially face onslaughts from other ideas. The challenge for believers in such a context is to consider and appreciate this reality.

It is presented to us in scripture when we are reminded that, "We are not of this world but we live in it." Paul's arrival in Athens as with every other city he travelled presented to him this reality that God ideas do not exist in a vacuum but face very realistic obstacles in the form of idols.

Mars Hill presented Paul with the opportunity to make a decision. How was he going to present and maintain the truth he preached in a context polluted by idols? Our natural inclination would have been to attack and confront the city with the truth, that it was perverse and poisoned by idolatry. Or we would flee and hide ourselves in a bid to preserve our purity. Yet, God worked in and through Paul in an amazing way to engage the culture of a city at its core.

When Paul entered Mars Hill he picked on the very things that the Athenians treasured; their idols (forms and ideas). He proceeded to present the truth in a way that was understandable for all who were listening.

Our 'postmodern' world is littered with idols and in many respects reflects the city of Athens. In our time people are in search of new ideas and solutions to life. The world's trust is in new technologies that should make life better and more efficient, better economic principles that will enhance our standard of living and better scientific research that will keep us younger and healthier for longer. Countless lives are reliant on these things.

So when a Christian is inspired by God to present a 'novel' way to live (the timeless gospel) it simultaneously courts suspicion and curiosity. There are some who will cynically ridicule the very notion of Christ and resurrection and then there are those who develop an interest in hearing something 'fresh' and unique. As Christians, we face the reality that the ideas God has given us will face the same challenges as Paul faced.

"Creating identification means taking the postmodern world seriously and addressing it from a collaborative rather than adversarial stance. A postmodern world demands a pulpit willing to be a viable conversation partner. In the words of one evangelical scholar, 'The challenge for the church is to claim this postmodern context for Christ." Preaching that recognizes and addresses the shifting idioms offers the world timeless good news of God's grace, love and provision." Localzo. C A. © 2000 with permission.

In saying this, Locazlo captures something of what Paul realized as a passionate carrier of God's ideas and intentions. Paul took the ideas and idols of Athens as something very serious in spite of the inherent falsehood. And instead of taking an adversarial stance or fleeing from idolatry, Paul chose to engage the philosophers of Mars Hill as viable conversation partners.

As believers, we too are challenged to take our current world as viable conversation partners. It is imperative that we take such a stance, so that we pursue to establish and express the kingdom of God to our current context. The timelessness of God ideas is captured in the relevance of the message of the cross to a given era.

Some historians believe that Paul standing on Mars Hill was a significant victory for the church, that amid the noisome voices of idolatry, Paul was able to clearly present the truth to his time.

According to T.R. Glover, in 435 AD or about 2 years later the Parthenon in Athens became a church and remained a church for a thousand years.

Instead of shunning and frowning arrogantly upon the idolatrous culture of the day, Paul engaged the culture of the day and the fruit thereof was seen in Athens for a thousand years. How will our engagement of this postmodern time reflect in a thousand years to come?

Chapter 9.

Workmanship of Christ

Eph 2:10

[10] For we are God's [own] handiwork (His workmanship), recreated in Christ Jesus, [born anew] that we may do those good works which God predestined (planned beforehand) for us [taking paths which He prepared ahead of time], that we should walk in them [living the good life which He prearranged and made ready for us to live]. AMP

Our perception of work is hinged entirely on what we term a career and job. Let us challenge this position by considering what it means to be Christ's workmanship. In life we have a path we may choose for ourselves

> **Key**
>
> All believers are an expression of God's handiwork.

based on our opinions, our parent's opinions or sometimes what is expected by society. Yet, Paul provides us with a reality of our unique state as creatures.

We must understand that as believers we are masterpieces of God's redemptive plan. We were first of all created according to Genesis that is, we were originally made in the image of God. But far more amazing is the fact that we have become new creatures through Christ Jesus. Paul's emphasis in this passage is that we are like poems or pieces of art in God's hand, not just functional beings but beautiful handiwork for display to heavenly rulers.

The cross presents a profound wonder of God's desire to redeem and save mankind. Salvation is more than just God's intention to restore function or moral right.

Rather, the cross is a reflection of the depth of God's love and the level of His creative and life giving power (Bara). The recreated human being is God's artistry in taking something that was dead and lifeless and transforming it into something that is purposeful and above all beautiful.

Furthermore, we were created for good works. These I believe aren't mere references to moral behavior but good works here make reference to every effort and endeavour of our lives in every area of human enterprise.

This is to say that God has predestined work for us in the families we live with, the peers we play and work with, the communities we interact in and the nations we live for and in. Our efforts to work (Good) stretch beyond being well behaved Christians, towards being very pragmatic and effective believers who not only preach the good news but also witness to the power of Christ to redeem and bring all things to himself.

"Purpose is not something merely discovered it is something that a man or woman must walk in." The African Knight

Ultimately, as the quote above states we are to thrive and walk in these good works. Our purpose in life is more than just a process of discovery and contemplation but, our purpose as the passage above clearly states is based on the good works God has predestined us to do and a clear instruction to walk in them.

Work as unto the Lord

Col 3:17

[17] And whatever you do [no matter what it is] in word or deed, do everything in the name of the Lord Jesus and in [dependence upon] His Person, giving praise to God the Father through Him. AMP

Obediently doing what is required of us.

Our deeds and words are an expression of God's will for the earth and all who are in it. When Jesus taught us to pray there are some significant points to highlight. (Matt 6:9-13 RSV)

Jesus taught us to welcome the kingdom of God and to submit and proclaim that God's total will be done on earth as his total will is done in heaven.

Our involvement in bringing or ushering in the kingdom of God (his rule and reign) and his supremacy and intentions (Your will be done) is revealed most importantly as we preach the gospel. And the fruit of the gospel are new disciples, not just converts.

Thus the impact of the gospel should reach and pervade all aspects of a person's life, so that his discipline (submission to Christ) should be revealed in all that a person does.

God is not only glorified when we sing songs and hymns but when we speak with clear and pure motives, when we do well and prove faithful and diligent in our work. God is glorified when we have good and wholesome fun.

God is glorified when we seek to better the life of another individual in need. "Whatever you do..." (Col 3:17 AMP) God ideas emerge out of individuals who are looking to glorify God essentially in everything that they do and say.

Most importantly, our work and efforts should be drawn out of total reliance on and in the power of Jesus Christ. Work as prescribed in this chapter should be an express desire and joy to display the wonder and goodness of God's will abounding and bearing fruit (good works) in the life of a believer. Everything we do will be evaluated in the end. (1 Cor 3:13 AMP)

Chapter 10.

Becoming vessels of God ideas – the Samaritan Strategy

Luke 10:33-35

But a certain Samaritan, as he traveled along, came down to where he was; and when he saw him, he was moved with pity and sympathy [for him],

34 And went to him and dressed his wounds, pouring on [them] oil and wine. Then he set him on his own beast and brought him to an inn and took care of him.

35 And the next day he took out two denarii [two day's wages] and gave [them] to the innkeeper, saying, Take care of him; and whatever more you spend, I [myself] will repay you when I return.
AMP

This parable shared by Jesus provides us with a unique and revolutionary way to extend and reveal the influence of God in our lives, communities and nations. At the heart of any God

> **Key**
>
> God expresses His love through the actions of believers.

idea is humble servitude to the needs of another person. Whether it affects Pharaoh or Darius (the kings of nations) or the wounded traveler, God ideas are a means and vehicle through which God may use us to help someone else.

The Samaritan is an expression of love in the harshest of environments. This story is told at a time when Jews hated their mixed blood brothers, such that the Samaritan represents at the time, a people group that was likened to dogs and was considered the lowest of the low.

Yet, even the lowest, despised and oppressed can serve. God ideas aren't limited to a special group of people but to everybody and anybody who willingly submits to the will of God.

There are a few things we can draw from this passage

Firstly, that we must by moved with sympathy and compassion by the plight of other people and people groups (nations). The Samaritan was a man driven by compassion. As he walked by the wounded man he was able to see the need that was evident. Compassion and sympathy will help us overcome the selfish blindness and myopia that limits us from any form of servitude.

Secondly, we must have a practical response for the given situation or a plan of action to respond to the situation. It is not enough for believers to see the plight that is so 'evident' in our world but we must also respond accordingly with God inspired practical action (God Ideas).

As the Samaritan reroutes his journey and puts the needs of the wounded man before his we learn something important about how we live our lives.

God ideas represent the effort we will make to assist and serve other people beyond our own personal needs. The Samaritan goes on to spend his time and money helping the wounded man.

Thirdly, through grace given by Christ we can go beyond the call of duty. Jesus talks about our expression of love to our families and those who love us as a natural and reciprocal act of duty. The Samaritan represents a man or woman who is willing to go beyond the natural call of duty.

The Samaritan spends his money and resources to ensure that the wounded man receives the necessary attention and is restored to health. As he leaves the injured man in the care of the inn keeper he makes a commitment to see the injured man reach full recovery.

Without an income and probably in a semi-conscious state the injured man would not have been able to meet the costs of recuperation. Knowing this the Samaritan stakes his word and name on all the costs the injured man will incur.

As we seek to do this, we become vessels of God's love and vehicles through which God can express His intentions and desires for people.

This story also echoes how Jesus says we should treat our enemies. There was definite and distinct enmity between the Jews and the Samaritans and Jesus was fully aware of this as He told the parable.

It supports the eight acts of unconditional love that we see in (Luke 6:27-38 RSV)

1. Love your enemies.
2. Do good to those who hate you.
3. Bless those who curse you.
4. Pray for those who persecute you.
5. Do not retaliate or fight back
6. Give freely and cheerfully.
7. Treat others the way you would want to be treated.
8. Judge not

The Samaritan reflects the nature and character of God and His love for all people more than the priest and the Levite who walked past the injured man consumed by their own piety. He goes beyond human nature and draws fully from the supernatural to effectively meet the needs of the wounded man.

Chapter 11.

The Bible gives us a wide and diverse range of aspects that reflect and present God's will and intentions to the world.

Lessons from the Old Testament
Affecting society as individuals.

The Old Testament provides a wide range of characters we have seen that were used by God to display His glory. Bezalel was a man empowered by the Spirit to become a

> **Key**
>
> We are called to affect society wit God Ideas.

skillful, intelligent and wise artisan with the ability to work, stone, wool, metal and other materials.

Noah was inspired to design and construct a phenomenal engineering and design feat. Daniel was used by God to display God's sovereignty over nations and the rulers as an astute and righteous politician.

Joseph served as a skilled governor who was used by God to bring a nation out of perilous crisis. Nehemiah served as a gifted project manager used by God to restore the honour and strength of a city and thus the honour of a nation.

Each of these characters was ordinary up until God got involved in their lives and spurred them on to greater exploits.

When we as individuals allow God's ideas to filter into our lives, we will become nothing less than great, for Paul clearly states that, "We are more than conquerors..." Daniel confidently proclaims that, "The people who know their God shall do great and mighty exploits."

Lessons from the New Testament

Affecting society as individuals and as a united community of believers.

In this modern time, the New Testament also reveals that we are not just individuals operating in isolation. Rather, we are a community of believers whom God is using to reveal Himself to the nations and principalities.

Paul's epistles reveal individuals and communities that are intent on revealing God's ideas to the nations.

From one city to the next (Philippi, Ephesus, Galatia) we encounter groups of believers being relevant and significant in their communities through the power of the Holy Spirit.

The New Testament provides a backdrop upon which God is painting a picture of the inherent and indwelling potential of every believer who chooses to pursue what they have been called and commissioned to pursue (the discipleship of all nations).

Paul makes very bold assertions pertaining to the new and dynamic state of the believer. He proclaims that the believer is a new creation, has all that pertains to life and godliness, displays the glory of God with increasing measure and intensity.

In Paul's eyes the cross is the all powerful and transforming work of God visible initially in man and ultimately in all creation.

The New Testament teaches us that the believer is beautiful work of art in the hands of God predestined to do good works and to walk in them for a lifetime.

Chapter 12.

As we pursue the ideas that God places in us, we will inevitably experience genuine and lasting revival as we experience transformation, reformation, conformation and

> **Key**
>
> God ideas revive all areas of society.

ultimately glorification. It will be revival that will affect our personal lives, influence our communal lives and affect nations and shape generations.

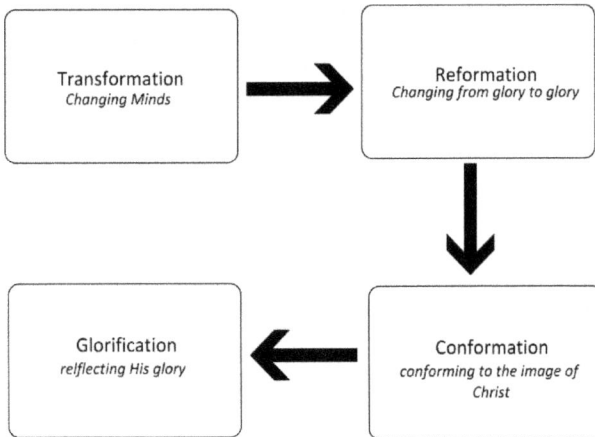

Figure 8 Ideas that glorify God - *Process of Revival*

God ideas bring revival

In personal life

Our personal lives as believers will be transformed immensely when we take time to seek first the kingdom of God and all its righteousness, in a bid to discover the ideas God has placed in us. If we pursue whole heartedly the God idea in us, we will discover and unlock the potential to transform and revive things in our daily lives.

We will have power from on high to do mighty exploits on behalf of God. When God's will is expressed through us, the world can only look in wonder and awe at the glory of God in plain and clear sight. (Rom2:1-2)

Whatever God is calling any believer to do, it is eternally significant, even if it may seem small and insignificant or ludicrous to the world at large (even to your family and friends like Joseph). The question remains and must be, (Zech 4:10) "Who despises the day of small beginnings?" No matter how small, weak and unnoticed we may be the most important thing is to be subject to God's will and intent. (1Cor 1:26-29; 1 Kings 19:11-13)

Our bodies and in fact our lives must be a living sacrifice to God and represent as Paul puts it, "A reasonable act of service and worship." Through this Paul is convinced that believers will embrace the opportunity to accept and nurture the new ideals and attitudes that come with salvation and submission to Christ.

In our bid to discover or pursue something unique or mind blowing we travel to different countries, embark on new initiatives. Yet we often miss out on the most amazing and breathtaking experience and change; change that happens when we embrace and surrender to the work of God in our hearts and minds.

> *"The longest journey one will travel is between heart and mind" The African Knight*

It is on this journey that the Word of God becomes so clear that as individuals we will know exactly what to do. Total surrender and the pursuit of the idea God has placed in you will,

- Put an end to the confusion that has plagued you for so long,
- Bring confirmation of what you were born to do,
- Unlock the passion welled up deep in your heart that is often misdirected and expressed as frustration and in worse cases desperation,
- And unlock true worship in its fullness. "I will bring you more than a song because a song in itself is not what you have required" says the worshiper.

Revival in families

The God idea brings about healthy and wholesome families where there is a glorious expression of all aspects of family.

22 Wives, be subject to your husbands, as to the Lord. 23 For the husband is the head of the wife as Christ is the head of the church, his body, and is himself its Savior. 24 As the church is subject to Christ, so let wives also be subject in everything to their husbands. RSV

In women it will bring about a glorious expression of being a wife and motherhood. It will be amazing to see wives totally submitted to their husbands as an act of love and commitment to a godly man not coerced subjugation.

The God idea for women in marriage is to view the husband in similar fashion to the way Christ is head of the church. Christ leads the church with grace, mercy and love as much as he rules with authority, justice and power.

So, a wife may look upon her husband in anticipation that he will represent and live for the home (family) with authority, justice and power mixed together so uniquely with abundant grace, mercy and love.

Or to see a husband who is genuinely affectionate to his wife.

Eph 5:25-33

25 Husbands, love your wives, as Christ loved the church and gave himself up for her, 26 that he might sanctify her, having cleansed her by the washing of water with the word, 27 that he might present the church to

himself in splendor, without spot or wrinkle or any such thing, that she might be holy and without blemish. 28 Even so husbands should love their wives as their own bodies. He who loves his wife loves himself. 29 For no man ever hates his own flesh, but nourishes and cherishes it, as Christ does the church, 30 because we are members of his body. 31 "For this reason a man shall leave his father and mother and be joined to his wife, and the two shall become one flesh." 32 This mystery is a profound one, and I am saying that it refers to Christ and the church; 33 however, let each one of you love his wife as himself, and let the wife see that she respects her husband. RSV

In men it will bring about a glorious expression of being a husband and fatherhood. The God idea for a man is to love his wife as Christ loved the church.

The responsibility of headship in the home carries the mantle of love and sacrifice that presents a spotless and beautiful bride. Much of what a husband is required to do is to ensure that a wife is loved and enjoys the privilege and joy of marriage.

God's intention for the man is to consider the implication and mystery of marital union which is that husband and wife become one flesh. It is in this that a husband is encouraged to care for and tend to his wife to the degree that Christ tends to the needs and desires of the church. Christ's relationship with the church is also sacrificial. Jesus Christ offered his life for the sake of the church. In so doing husbands like Christ will enjoy the splendor of a sanctified (set apart) woman. As a man loves his wife as Christ loves the church, he creates the right environment for her purity and loveliness to increase with time. (Prov 31: 30-31)

It is in such an environment that obedient children can be raised.

Eph 6:1-4

6 Children, obey your parents in the Lord, for this is right. 2 "Honor your father and mother" (this is the first commandment with a promise), 3 "that it may be well with you and that you may live long on the earth." 4 Fathers, do not provoke your children to anger, but bring them up in the discipline and instruction of the Lord. RSV

In an age where rebellion is rife among children, it will be glorious to see children who eagerly obey their parents as a means to please the Lord. Parents have the express opportunity to raise children who will live long because the have been taught to honour and obey.

The family is the seedbed upon which nations and communities can bring about generational transformation as they pass on instruction and a standard of life based on clear instruction and training in God. Obedient children who honour their parents will also find favour and long life. It's amazing how obedience honour can affect the demographics and economies of a nation over generations.

Finally, it will be wonderful to see a family where fathers rather than provoke or irritate their children, affirm them in God so as to motivate children to higher and more purposeful living. When we see families that truly express the leadership and love of God there will be a glorious expression of God ideas in other areas of life.

Revival in the workplace

Col 3:22-4:1

> [22]Servants, obey in everything those who are your earthly masters, not only when their eyes are on you as pleasers of men, but in simplicity of purpose [with all your heart] because of your reverence for the Lord and as a sincere expression of your devotion to Him. [23] Whatever may be your task, work at it heartily (from the soul), as [something done] for the Lord and not for men, [24] Knowing [with all certainty] that it is from the Lord [and not from men] that you will receive the inheritance which is your [real] reward. [The One Whom] you are actually serving [is] the Lord Christ (the Messiah). [25] For he who deals wrongfully will [reap the fruit of his folly and] be punished for his wrongdoing. And [with God] there is no partiality [no matter what a person's position may be, whether he is the slave or the master].

> Chapter 4

> [1] MASTERS, [on your part] deal with your slaves justly and fairly, knowing that also you have a Master in heaven. [Lev 25:43,53.] AMP

As people pursue the God idea in them, the work place will be transformed by the passion to please Jesus. Even the menial tasks frowned upon by all men, like cleaning and maintenance will be performed to such excellence that God is glorified.

The marketplace will be vibrant as people express the essence of true economics, when they responsibly manage resources as bosses because they are in full submission and surrender to their master in heaven.

A nation's economy will thrive because of industrious people eager to bring glory to their Father in heaven. If believers unleash the God idea resident in them for the market place we will see an increase and multiplication in fruitfulness in everything from profit, to performance and even motivation. We will see innovation occurring as employees and bosses alike are inspired to move from one glory to the next in their work life.

Rom 13:8-10

[8]Keep out of debt and owe no man anything, except to love one another; for he who loves his neighbor [who practices loving others] has fulfilled the Law [relating to one's fellowmen, meeting all its requirements].

[9] The commandments, You shall not commit adultery, You shall not kill, You shall not steal, You shall not covet (have an evil desire), and any other commandment, are summed up in the single command, You shall love your neighbor as [you do] yourself. [Ex 20:13-17; Lev 19:18.][10] Love does no wrong to one's neighbor [it never

hurts anybody]. Therefore love meets all the requirements and is the fulfilling of the Law. AMP

Believers will in light of growing consumerism and growth of individual and national debt, aspire to develop an economy where people work together and live within their means. It will be a place where the only thing that someone must owe is the expression and extension of love and compassion to their neighbor.

Revival in Community

Rom 12:9-21

> 9 Let love be genuine; hate what is evil, hold fast to what is good; 10 love one another with brotherly affection; outdo one another in showing honor. 11 Never flag in zeal, be aglow with the Spirit, serve the Lord. 12 Rejoice in your hope, be patient in tribulation, be constant in prayer. 13 Contribute to the needs of the saints, practice hospitality.
>
> 14 Bless those who persecute you; bless and do not curse them. 15 Rejoice with those who rejoice, weep with those who weep. 16 Live in harmony with one another; do not be haughty, but associate with the lowly; never be conceited. 17 Repay no one evil for evil, but take thought for what is noble in the sight of all. 18 If possible, so far as it depends upon you, live peaceably with all.
>
> 19 Beloved, never avenge yourselves, but leave it to the wrath of God; for it is written, "Vengeance is mine, I will repay, says the Lord." 20 No, "if your enemy is hungry, feed him; if he is thirsty, give him drink; for by so doing you will heap burning coals upon his head." 21 Do not be overcome by evil, but overcome evil with good. RSV

At the heart of a God idea is genuine love for other people; an unflinching devotion to the restoration of an individual or the community at large. The greatest service we offer the Lord is when we seek to meet the needs of other people less privileged than ourselves.

Furthermore, we are challenged also, to endeavour to do good for our enemies. A humble and contrite heart can turn the hardest of hearts into soft and warm flesh. Our communities will thrive on compassion as believers seek to serve and better the life of their fellow man.

The God idea seeks to lift up the down trodden, bind up the broken hearted, bring good news to the poor. Our eyes will not be blind to the plight and hardship abundantly evident in a fallen world. Communities will be a place where people aren't condemned but are loved to such an extent that they cannot deny the existence and glory of God.

There will be such a hunger for the gospel that brings salvation that the four walls of the church will have to be broken down countless times for more people to receive the abundant love of Christ.

Mother Theresa says this, "At the end of life, we will not be judged by how many diplomas we received, how much money we have made, how many great things we have done. We will be judged by [the words of Jesus], 'I was hungry and you gave me something to eat, I was naked and you clothed me. I was homeless and you took me in' (Mt 25:35 RSV)... the poor are Christ in distressing disguise." Miller et al (pg 5, 2005)

God ideas reveal to us the growing need in our communities for the love of Christ whether it is the poor or the people we despise and hate. We must as Paul so rightly states, "Not be overcome by evil but to overcome [defeat] evil with good." As we do this, we will see our communities reflecting more of Christ and thereby our hopes and dreams for nations become evermore clearer.

In nations

Rom 13:1-7

> [1] LET EVERY person be loyally subject to the governing (civil) authorities. For there is no authority except from God [by His permission, His sanction], and those that exist do so by God's appointment. [Prov 8:15.] [2]Therefore he who resists and sets himself up against the authorities resists what God has appointed and arranged [in divine order]. And those who resist will bring down judgment upon themselves [receiving the penalty due them].

> [3] For civil authorities are not a terror to [people of] good conduct, but to [those of] bad behavior. Would you have no dread of him who is in authority? Then do what is right and you will receive his approval and commendation.

> [4] For he is God's servant for your good. But if you do wrong, [you should dread him and] be afraid, for he does not bear and wear the sword for nothing. He is God's servant to execute His wrath (punishment,

132

vengeance) on the wrongdoer. [5] Therefore one must be subject, not only to avoid God's wrath and escape punishment, but also as a matter of principle and for the sake of conscience.

[6]For this same reason you pay taxes, for [the civil authorities] are official servants under God, devoting themselves to attending to this very service. [7] Render to all men their dues. [Pay] taxes to whom taxes are due, revenue to whom revenue is due, respect to whom respect is due, and honor to whom honor is due. AMP

Difficult as it may seem for believers to obey and be subject to rulers and leaders of nations (especially in nations with bad governments, autocratic or otherwise).

Paul advocates for believers to humbly subject themselves to authorities as a matter of obedience to God. It is interesting to note that Paul says that all authority is God ordained or designed and serves a specific purpose within His plan. He goes so far as to say those who resist civil authority risk going against God's plan.

Yet on the other hand, he does not advocate total silence in the face of injustice and oppression. Believers are in a precarious yet gracious position to model good citizenship within a nation state.

As with the example of Daniel, they carry the responsibility of serving and being diligent stewards (even within a despotic monarchy or government). Yet, when it is required of them to speak, they must present the truth according to God's word. It is the same with Paul who in many respects maintained the law of the land, yet didn't shrink back when he was required to preach the good news. (Acts 20:27) In Acts 26 when Paul was to defend his life he went on to present the Gospel to King Agrippa with such intensity that Agrippa was concerned that in his defense Paul was trying to convert him to Christianity.

Because believers are obedient to the will of God and honour government (Romans 13) and civil authority rather than antagonize, we will see opportunity for more truth to be spoken in the halls of politics and governance.

As believers represent the King of kings, there will be more opportunity to bring about reformation so that, where there's no equity believers can speak audibly with their voices and actions to shed light on wickedness. It will be to such a degree that it commands repentance, lest a man falls deeper into wickedness and reprobate thinking.

As God gets involved in a nation's governance and political structures, we will see more glimpses of God's government that will be reflected through believers acting justly and civilly, rendering to all men their dues, to Caesar what belongs to Caesar whilst rendering to God what belongs to God; the hearts of redeemed men.

In Generations

2 Tim 1:3-5

3 I thank God whom I serve with a clear conscience, as did my fathers, when I remember you constantly in my prayers. 4 As I remember your tears, I long night and day to see you, that I may be filled with joy. 5 I am reminded of your sincere faith, a faith that dwelt first in your grandmother Lo'is and your mother Eunice and now, I am sure, dwells in you. RSV

As believers in an age pursue God ideas, they will not have to worry about future generations because they will have built upon a firm and unshakable foundation, which is Christ Jesus.

Paul clearly recognizes that Timothy possessed the faith that was clearly evident in his grandmother and also in his mother. This passage represents the generational impact of the gospel.

Families, communities and nations will not be built on temporal ideas and philosophies that lead to death but will be built on the firm foundation of God's enduring word.

There will be a loud proclamation throughout nations and generations, "As for me and my house we shall serve the Lord." (Josh 24:15 RSV)

In the book of Revelation there is a glorious image of a multitude of people praising and worshiping God. (see Rev 7: 9-11 RSV)

This image is a reflection of countless people in an age that chose the narrower and more difficult task of forsaking temporal pleasures for the glory of a future kingdom.

The multitude in heaven is a direct result of each generation of believers committing to serve ideas that bring reformation, transformation and ultimately bring glory to God.

Chapter 13.

The God Idea in You

"If we do not disciple the nations the nations will disciple us." Anon

The day that you received Christ as your Lord and Saviour, something happened internally that cannot be changed; you were justified before God. Justification is more than an event it is a state and disposition that translates to all aspects of your life. This means that in terms of work, family, recreation, education and all other aspects of life, you have access to the throne of God, where you can seek the best way to live your life.

Salvation means that you no longer have to wander or wonder aimlessly, but you can receive direction and clear insight into what you were born to do and who you were born to be. As the God idea permeates your life, your significance will be derived from God and His view of you, rather than from how much you've acquired or lost.

The God idea in you is the Holy Spirit causing you to will and to act according to the will of the Father in heaven. (Phil 2:13 RSV)

There is nothing more glorious than all the faculties of a man being used to the glory of God. It is more than songs and preaching confined to the four walls of a building. It is when God's will is made known to the world through all possible avenues. It is when God's manifold wisdom is expressed in the life of the church (corporate and individual) to the principalities. Furthermore, it's God's bara (creative power) working in and through the life of every believer.

Each and every believer is in possession of great GOD IDEAS that will ultimately result in actions that will glorify God. And there are 3 inherent things to appreciate about every believer.

Passion

There is something that you are definitely passionate about. You enjoy it secretly or publicly but one thing is certain you would do it whether someone paid you for it or not. Oftentimes whatever it is, it's like the word of God pent up like a fire in Jeremiah's bones, as much as you hold back you want to do it for God's glory. (Jer 20: 9 RSV)

Whenever you think of this, it burns in you what I often call the Burning Passion Factor BPF. Key to releasing and enjoying God ideas is the passion to do something for God. God ideas are revealed when you are able to say, "Here I am send me..." (Isa 6: 8 RSV) when God is needs someone to send.

Impact

As many times as you do whatever you're passionate about, it makes a significant impact on others. The world has taught us to look at impact as something grand but, I believe that impact is when a believer does something that God has instructed, no matter how insignificant it seems. God ideas may not be grand in their impact to the naked eye but will always be grand in the spiritual, especially in God's eyes. Fulfilling and committing to doing the will of God presents the express opportunity for a believer to do and say things that will impact the present age as well as the eternal age to come.

Belief

No matter how much anyone downplays whatever you love to do, deep down somewhere in your heart and mind you believe you can do it. God ideas are built on a resilient and sustaining faith. Every human being has been wired to believe or to have faith; the challenge will always be experiencing the full and glorious expression of faith. For believers this means when God tells you that you can part the Red Sea you stand atop a rock and you raise your staff. Such faith represents the conviction in your heart of who you rely on and trust.

Ultimately, you must realize that you carry the power of God which, Paul calls treasure in clay jars (2 Cor 4:7 RSV). This treasure is a wonderful opportunity and privilege for us as believers to participate in God's work to redeem and gather all things back to Him by revealing this treasure. Ultimately, we will progress forward towards permanently and perfectly reflecting God's glory for eternity. (fig 9 below)

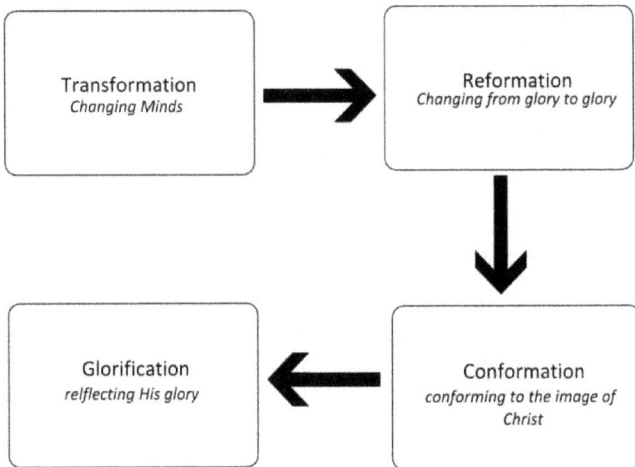

Figure 9 Ideas that glorify God - *Result of God ideas*

I must at this point courageously veer from the beaten track of this book and add a very personal testament that has inspired me. I met a woman in Harare who inspired me greatly.

She is a woman with a vision to reach the orphaned and vulnerable children with the gospel of Jesus expressed in art. Simplistic and small as this seems, it has immense and significant effects on eternity, if we consider that each time she wins over a soul in an orphanage, legions upon legions of angels celebrate.

More importantly her compassion and love infectiously rubbed off onto other Christians who in turn will seek to release their God given vision and passion.

I was one of those Christians inspired by this woman and she has significantly contributed to this book in ways she may have never imagined and so I thought to dedicate a paragraph of this book to her. Thank you Sharon Sevenzo!

Chapter 14.

God's surpassing glory in you.

2 Cor 3: 10, 18; Heb 1:2; Matt 5:14; Psalm 97

The effects and active pursuit of God ideas is for the believer to reveal and radiate God's glory to all people. When believers truly serve God's intentions in any given arena they will effectively radiate

> **Key**
>
> God ideas express and display God's glory to the world.

God's glory. God's glory is effectively the inner working of God's power transforming the heart and mind of the believer. As a believer 'mirror' images what the word of God says to the world with boldness and unveiled face something significant happens.

Firstly, the believer is progressively transformed into the likeness of Christ with increasing measure. Transformed as I shared earlier in the book is from the Greek word that means metamorphosis, a change from inside out. We are transfigured into the likeness of Christ is putting it in another way.

Secondly, believers radiate the glory of God with ever increasing measure to the world. Paul says that we have received is permanent and of surpassing splendor to what Moses received when he ascended the mountain to meet with the Lord.

Hence, as believers we radiate with ever increasing luminance the wonderful light and glory of our Saviour Jesus when we pursue and fulfill His will and intentions in the entirety of our lives.

What happens when we reflect and radiate the glory of God?

Inevitably, the poor will hear the good news; the captives will be set free, those who are blind will see, those who are unwell are healed and those who were dead come to life. As believers pursue a God idea they proclaim the year of the Lord's favour!

God's glory then reflects in the church on a Sunday morning and overflows and reflects in other areas of life such as economics, politics, health, education and every other cultural endeavour of man. As believers proclaim the year of the Lord's favour nations must see a genuine expression of God's favour as it is radiated by believers.

When God's glory was with Moses and the children of Israel, it not only shaped for the lack of a better word the 'religious' practice of Israel, it shaped every other aspect of life.

God's presence and glory served to shape the destiny of a nation. Israel's politics, economics and health were shaped by God's presence in the land. As long as God was with them and they were attentive and obedient to His instruction they found favour with Him in all respects.

Yet, Paul says that Moses who encountered more deeply the splendor and glory of God had a fading experience; it was temporary.

Believers in Jesus however have a surpassing glory which is permanent. Paul continues and proclaims that we have hope and certainty in the fact that we have received this surpassing glory that gives us a reason to be bold. We are, to boldly (unveiled faces) reveal the word of God in all its glory, wisdom and splendor to all people and nations. As we engage our cultures, different world views and ideologies, believers have the capacity and power to reveal God ideas (what He originally intended in the beginning and what His ultimate intentions are),

- A glorified man at the heart of the new creation,
- God building a new city with glorified inhabitants,
- His will to establish a new heaven and new earth,
- Christ's intent to present a perfect bride (glorified church).

As we fix our eyes on fulfilling God ideas we will be radiating God's glory to the nations and we will see different aspects of our nations and communities transformed and revived by the word of God.

Chapter 15.

Becoming a part of God's Economy

1 Peter 4:10

10 As each has received a gift, employ it for one another, as good stewards of God's varied grace: RSV

It is important to appreciate that we need to be involved in whatever God is doing in the world. And to become a part of this, we need to understand what is happening in the world around us. I have picked my context to help us appreciate

> **Key**
>
> Problems and challenges are opportunities to reveal God ideas.

the necessity and importance of God Ideas in the times we are living in. Below, are some statistics relating to Africa's problems as presented by Hein Van Wyk in his seminar on the need for a biblical world view in Africa.

- Gross National & Gross Domestic Product
  - 17 of poorest 21 countries in Africa

- Infant Mortality Rate

  - 148 out of every 1,000 children, who survive birth, will die before age of five.
  - Life Expectancy and Literacy
  - Life Expectancy in 2000 = 50 years
  - 29 of lowest 42 countries found in Africa

- HIV/AIDS Infection Rate

  - *71% of World's HIV/AIDS cases in Africa*
  - *6,000 people die each day*
  - *12 million HIV/AIDS Orphans; 20 million in 2010*
  - *HIV/AIDS infected people in Africa 28.5 million*
- Heavily Indebted Poor Countries (HIPC)
  - *30 of 42 countries eligible for HIPC in Africa*

- Human Development Index (HDI)

  - *HDI attempts to measure "Quality of Life"*
  - *Composite of four criteria:*
    - Life expectancy
    - Literacy rates
    - Educational attainment
    - Adjusted real income
  - *174 countries qualified; 33 of bottom 40 are in Africa*
    - Least Developed Countries Index (LDC)
  - *34 of 50 least developed countries are in Africa.*

- Human Suffering Index (HIS)
  - *24 out of 30 countries described as "extreme human suffering" are in Africa*

- Corruption Perception Index (CPI)
  - *52 out of 102 in the highly corrupt range of the index; 16 are in Africa*
- Index of Economic Freedom
  - *Of the 71 countries rated "mostly un-free", 30 are from Africa.*
- Freedom Index

- 55 countries, including 21 from Africa are "partially free". 40 countries, including 20 from Africa, are not free.
 - 21 World Crises identified by the United Nations as effecting 45 million people
   - 17 of the 21 are in Africa

For many of us these merely represent inherent and stark problems, but I believe in the eyes of a believer totally submitted to the will of God, they represent boundless opportunities to bring about transformation and the glory of God. Our bold and courageous proclamation of faith must be… "Your will be done on earth as it is in heaven. " (Matt 6:10 RSV)

We must appreciate that we are God's servants and labourers or more clearly God's household managers. When God gives us ideas and directs our paths, it is clearly for a bigger and more significant purpose; even when we perform a very small task like giving $1 under God's instruction.

The problems faced by Africa look large and insurmountable when we consider them broadly. But, if we appreciate that each problem reflects the attitude and perspectives of an individual, we can then see different opportunities and ways to address them.

As stewards of God's resources we can then make commitments to change the world one person at a time starting with ourselves.

"Transformation takes place when a new worldview replaces an old one."—William Miller

Key things to establish in God's economy

Importantly, we must take some things into consideration as we begin to serve God's intentions.

1. **Surrender** – humbly presenting all, everything to Jesus. Total surrender to the will and power of God.
2. **Faith** – total assurance of the things that are unseen and the substance or essence of what we hope for.
3. **Wisdom** – reverence of the Lord. Fearing him in worship and awe.
4. **Grace** – unmerited and underserved favour freely and eagerly expressed in the lives of believers.
5. **Trust** – when things remain unclear and uncertain the ability to continue accepting that God is sovereign and in control.
6. **Perseverance** – resolute and unwavering pursuit of a desired goal.
7. **Vision** – a picture or glimpse of the future.

What is God intent on doing in the world today?

Without a doubt, God is extending His rule and reign. God's intent is a clear and consistent thread throughout scripture and throughout time that His name is glorified above all other names.

It is also evident that His rule and reign be established throughout the world as it says in (Revelation 11:15 RSV), "Now the kingdoms of this world are now the kingdoms of our God and His Christ." God is interested in ruling every area of human thought, endeavour and activity.

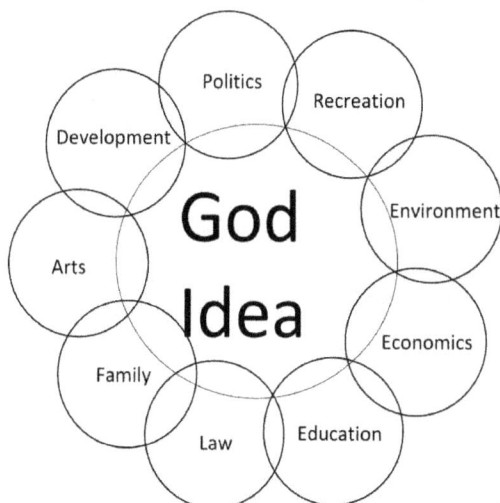

Figure 10 God Ideas spreading - *The redemptive plan*

His redemptive plan (figure 10)

Politics: Consider (Isa 9:6 RSV) "...and the government shall be on his shoulders." Our involvement in politics is to remind the kings and leaders of our time that they are also under a sovereign God.

It is to reveal to them their responsibility is to govern well with justice and equity as individuals ordained by God to lead.

Like Daniel and Joseph who were involved in the politics of the day, we must confess the truth of God and act accordingly with reverence and submission to God so as to show our leaders that God delights in mercy and in people who act justly. Furthermore, we must consider how Paul engaged the men of Mars hill as a means to challenge the ideologies of the day. Be it autocracy or democracy, as believers we have the opportunity to engage politics so as to reveal the government and rule of our Lord Jesus Christ on earth.

Development: When God gave Adam the mandate to be fruitful and to multiply and subdue the earth it had no specified cap or limit. It must follow therefore that our present systems don't align to God's original intention because there are some who have and some who have not. With tireless zeal we must endeavour to restore human dignity and to responsibly draw resources from the earth. Thereby developing a sustainable system of livelihood that provides for everybody, while preserving the resources we have on earth.

God is calling us to be diligent household managers who endeavour to meet and serve the needs of other people whilst responsibly dealing with His creation according to his original mandate.

Recreation: We must always remember that there is joy in the Holy Spirit and in God's kingdom. It is imperative that we also learn to have fun, to laugh and enjoy the life that God has given us. The world is filled with so much that can bring joy and pleasure without infringing on our relationship with God. God has created for us the basic units to make music, make pictures with colour, ingredients to make good food, a world full of beauty and diversity and the power of genuine and intelligent interaction.

Family – God made us social creatures and so inevitably granted us families to live in. God's will is to see families restored and the bonds of fellowship between members of a family being strongly rooted in unconditional love.

Education – we must endeavour to establish an environment for learning in our communities. Learning will contribute to ending poverty but will also ensure that everybody has a trade they can use to contribute to the development of a nation. Believers must work to nurture a sense of dignity that will allow people to discover their capacity to function and serve as stewards of God's resources.

The Arts – As we celebrate beauty and the honourable things in life, the arts must provide us with a relevant and positive interpretation of creation and also human cultures. The artist must contribute to the development of perspectives.

Like education the artist can also provide an understanding of life that contributes to positive changes and transformation in local and global cultures.

The artist has within him/her the capacity to present fresh and powerful ideas that will help to redeem the wonderful God-given aspects of a culture.

The Environment – God's will is to see man subdue the earth to make it fruitful by using it wisely. Our challenge is to ensure that we continue to manage the earth's resources well and that we continue to ensure that the earth can be fruitful from seed time to harvest.

More so, continually seeking to produce renewable energy sources and sustainable solutions that ensure that the earth will continue to produce, multiply and sustain human and creature existence.

Paul in (Romans 1:20 RSV) presents to us the depth of God's involvement in creation (His Immanence). This verse shows us that there is a reflection of God in creation that must be honoured and respected.

We are to be faithful stewards and managers of all that God has made.

Law – It will be amazing to see communities that reflect the reality of being under the grace of God. It is God's will to see a free society where there are less and less repressive and interventionist laws.

These societies will reflect the deeper more profound realities of freedom as rights and expression will be built on the ineffable responsibility to love one's neighbor.

Importantly, we will see a society that establishes legislation that is reformative in nature. From the criminal justice system to civil society, God's will is to see more love between people and work to bind up the broken hearted, release from darkness those that are in prison.

Economics – Ultimately to see the rise of the household steward in economies that is to say, people who will responsibly manage what they have received from God. Critically, we will see households and firms dealing in equity.

Nation's built on hard work and equity will emerge to reveal the wonder of a man or woman who excels in doing all things as unto the Lord.

The basic definition of economics will have to be challenged to focus primarily on needs before focusing on wants. Hence, policy on a national level will be challenged to prioritize what is beneficial and altogether sustainable for the broad populace.

Chapter 16.

Coram Deo

Coram Deo is a Latin phrase that captures an ongoing and unending reality for all human activity under the sun. The reality is this that all human beings live under the watchful eye of God and will ultimately be

> **Key**
>
> We can draw on God's wisdom for every aspect of life.

answerable to Him for their actions and specifically their life choices.

Coram Deo means that life is lived before the face of God. In all endeavours and aspects of life the believer lives, in the presence of, under the authority of; and to the glory and honour of God.

Heb 4:13

13 And not a creature exists that is concealed from His sight, but all things are open and exposed, naked and defenseless to the eyes of Him with Whom we have to do. AMP

For believers it is necessary to actually enjoy and embrace this reality as it presents the wondrous opportunity to enter into God's throne room and draw upon God's limitless stores of grace and mercy.

One reason why Jesus teaches us to seek the kingdom of God and its righteousness before anything else (Matt 6:33 RSV), is that we can then see the rest of the world and its circumstances as a canvas upon which God can use our temporary situations as paint to display the beauty of eternal life.

Furthermore, for believers, it is an opportunity to gather wisdom and understanding from the one who knows all things. All problems and situations in different societies have solutions.

Coram Deo must with all certainty become a lifestyle of service, as each encounter with the Living God changes the hearts and minds of believers thereby affecting the communities and nations believers live in.

As believers spend time in God's presence they will inevitably discover what, 'breaks' God's heart in a specific community or nation.

Living before the face of God means that believers can discover what God knows about His creation, which is everything and thus serve as messengers (Ambassadors) who deliver God's will and love to the nations.

Chapter 17.

Building with the end (beginning) in mind

Finally, in a bid to be fully effective in this world, believers must have a long term focus and view based on the future determined in the Bible.

> **Key**
>
> We need to live by design, with the end in mind.

Much of our planning, motives, goals and objectives must be based upon the clear notion that history as we know it will come to an end. It is from this basis that we will appreciate the wonder of living by design (telos).

The scripture below reveals the truth that the earth and heaven we know will pass away and there will be a new heaven and new earth. In the midst of this newness will be New Jerusalem (a new city).

Rev 21:1-4

21 Then I saw a new heaven and a new earth; for the first heaven and the first earth had passed away, and the sea was no more. 2 And I saw the holy city, new

Jerusalem, coming down out of heaven from God, prepared as a bride adorned for her husband;

3 and I heard a loud voice from the throne saying, "Behold, the dwelling of God is with men. He will dwell with them, and they shall be his people, and God himself will be with them; 4 he will wipe away every tear from their eyes, and death shall be no more, neither shall there be mourning nor crying nor pain any more, for the former things have passed away." RSV

God ideas are entrenched in a strong sense of eternity and the reality that Christ will return. Christ's glorious return will usher in a great celebration and will also perfectly restore the relationship between God and man.

As believers capture a vision of this glorious and breathtaking end, they will hunger to share and witness this reality in as many ways and places as possible, doing all things as unto the Lord (Col 3: 17 paraphrased RSV).

As believers pursue God ideas they will in due course impact eternity. We are to commit ourselves as believers to thoughts, passions, endeavors and activities that will affect eternity, according to the salvation we have received. If we truly submit to God we will see a future shaped by God's righteousness and grace. It is this future that we should aspire to attain and fulfill.

At the very end of time we will discover the purpose of our lives, to know Him fully as we are fully known.

(1 Cor 13:12 paraphrased RSV) Paul presents such a profound reality when he says, "We shall know him in full." It is amazing to think that we shall see God in all his unfathomable fullness as the angels do now.

Our work on this earth and pursuit of God Ideas will lead us to glorification, when Christ makes all things new and perfect.

C.S. Lewis talks about this in his book Mere Christianity that, Jesus is intent on making us perfect; nothing less will do for Him. He is intent on having a beautiful bride (the church). This church (New Jerusalem) is a beautifully adorned dwelling place for the presence of God. Furthermore, it is a place where man can once more dwell in perfect harmony with God.

Rev 21:24-27

24 By its light shall the nations walk; and the kings of the earth shall bring their glory into it, 25 and its gates shall never be shut by day - and there shall be no night there;

26 they shall bring into it the glory and the honor of the nations. 27 But nothing unclean shall enter it, nor any one who practices abomination or falsehood, but only those who are written in the Lamb's book of life. RSV

Much of what God will have done through His people will be revealed in the glorious Holy city. The God ideas that will have served to transform and redeem an individual, a community and a nation's culture will be seen as each tribe and tongue enter into the city. I believe verse 26 reveals the depth of transformation that will be experienced as nations (different tribes and countries) their diversity and uniqueness in the city. There is a mystery to this, as the Bible states that we are all one new man in Christ yet we remain ethnically and culturally diverse in our expression of the new work of Christ.

Hence, all that has been purified by the work of Christ through believers will be seen in the city and all those whose lives were purchased by the blood of Lamb that was slain will also be revealed.

Rev 7:9-11

After this I looked, and behold, a great multitude which no man could number, from every nation, from all tribes and peoples and tongues, standing before the throne and before the Lamb, clothed in white robes, with palm branches in their hands, 10 and crying out with a loud voice, "Salvation belongs to our God who sits upon the throne, and to the Lamb!" RSV

As each individual, church and community embrace and receive God ideas that express and reveal His will, they serve to meet and embrace eternal life and the glory of the new heaven, earth and city to come.

Believers will be a supporting response in modern times to the faith that was in the age old heroes of faith, who looked forward to a city with foundations, whose architect and builder is God.

Heb 11:8-11

8 By faith Abraham obeyed when he was called to go out to a place which he was to receive as an inheritance; and he went out, not knowing where he was to go. 9 By faith he sojourned in the land of promise, as in a foreign land, living in tents with Isaac and Jacob, heirs with him of the same promise. 10 For he looked forward to the city which has foundations, whose builder and maker is God. RSV

Believers will become people who seek to attain to God's great design for all creation. We will become a glorified and perfect reflection of God's intent from the beginning. There's nothing as fulfilling as knowing that one lived for something greater, for God's ultimate purpose.

Definition of telos

Telos (tel'-os); from a primary tello (to set out for a definite point or goal); properly, the point aimed at as a limit, i.e. (by implication) the conclusion of an act or state (termination [literally, figuratively or indefinitely], result [immediate, ultimate or prophetic], purpose); specifically, an impost or levy (as paid):

(Biblesoft's New Exhaustive Strong's Numbers and Concordance with Expanded Greek-Hebrew Dictionary. Copyright © 1994, 2003, 2006 Biblesoft, Inc. and International Bible Translators, Inc.)

Reflections

As I consider this material, my thoughts turn to my ever present context of Africa and its burgeoning needs. More than ever, Africa is in desperate need of a generation of young men and women who carry God ideas for the nations of this continent. And there is a pertinent need to give thought to certain things.

Much of what God calls us to do within communities and nations as believers is built upon the word of our testimony and the active outworking of our faith. The final reflections are a collection of tools to help us consider the testimony we possess and the effectiveness of the actions we perform to reflect or express our faith.

There are four final reflections that represent four key aspects that I believe are relevant to practical action namely analysis, methodology, applied learning and views of life.

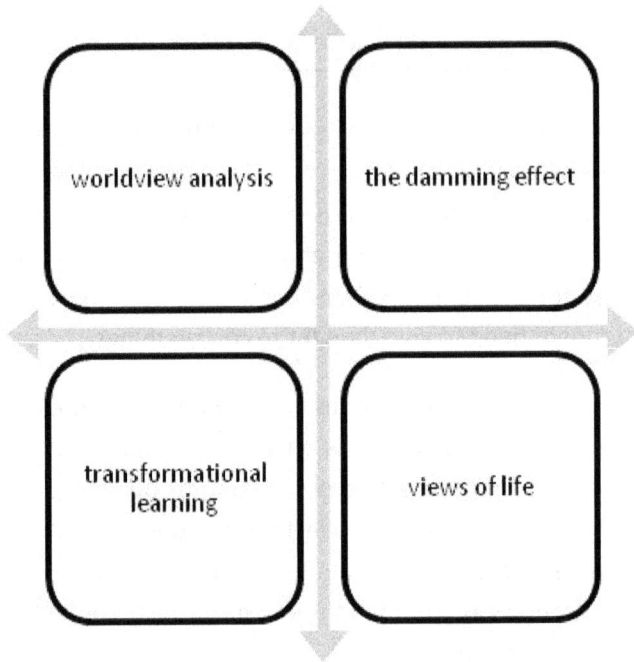

Figure 11 Four Reflections

They are not entirely exhaustive and represent my personal reflections and study. My hope is that they serve to inspire further reflection, study and active response to what God has so keenly deposited in every believer as a guarantee, the Holy Spirit which is the power that raised Christ from the dead.

Reflection One

A cultural mandate

Worldview analysis –

God ideas do not operate in a vacuum and they are generally predisposed to a specific cultural context. So before implementing a God idea, it is important to assess and appreciate the prevailing worldview in light of the broader cultural context you live in e.g.

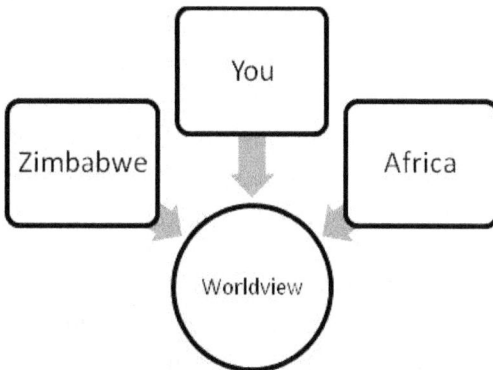

Figure 12 Worldview Context

There are 3 levels to consider

1. What are the key drivers of worldview and culture in your current context?
2. What are the key perspectives and perceptions you have of the world and reality?
3. What is the expression of culture and worldview (behavior) within your society?

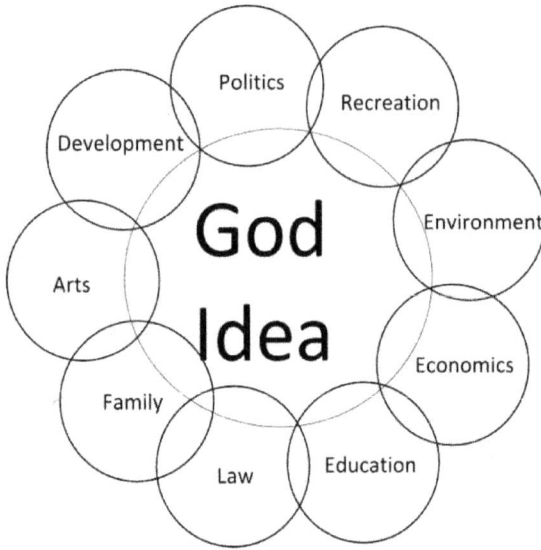

Figure 13 God Ideas spreading

It is at these 3 levels that we must work through 4 key perspectives that form the foundation of what we value. Try to answer the following questions;

1. What is your ultimate reality? i.e.
   a. What is the basis of your faith?
   b. What do you really believe?
2. What is the nature of nature? i.e.
   a. What is your view of resources, the world and nature in general?
   b. What is you view of the environment around you
3. What is the nature of man? i.e.
   a. What is your view of people especially in your community?
   b. What do you think are the basic belief systems in your community?

c. What is/are the cultural myth(s) that contribute to moral, spiritual, intellectual, political, medical, economic or social poverty in your community
4. Where is history going?
   a. What is your perspective of the past, present and future?
   b. What do you appreciate about the time period you're living in?

Essentially, as we analyze and question your world view, you're appreciating the combined and systematic effect of natural cause and effect and the intervention of the supernatural and divine in the progression and consequence of history.

c. What do you understand to be the facts and determinants of the past, present and the future of your community?
d. **Discovery:** What do you think is worthwhile? I.e.
e. What is life giving and fulfilling to you?

Above in the diagram (Fig 13) are the key drivers of culture that form the expression of what we believe and engender as values. Failure to look into these matters will always keep problems looking bigger than they are. No problem is bigger than God.

Illumina (Tyndale house Publishers 2002 www.tyndale.com) propose seven steps that are helpful when engaging culture,

Acts 17:33-34

From Paul's approach to the Athenians, we find some great pointers on how to approach a culture that takes itself far too seriously. The way to win some is to be **winsome:**

1. Watch for ways to find common ground (Acts 17:22-23).
   - Paul went where people were physically and began where they were intellectually.
2. Illuminate poor views of God (Acts 17:24-26).
   - Paul gently but firmly exposed the errant views of the Athenians. There is a knowable God. On that front they were wrong and needed correction.
3. Nurture that part of each person that wants to know God (Acts 17:27).
   - Paul knew that there is a God-built part of every person that wants to know God. When we talk to those who don't know God, we need to assume this and nurture it.
4. Study the world and its ways (Acts 17:28-30).
   - Paul was a student of the culture. Christians tend to isolate, insulate, run and hide, gather up in our holy huddle and avoid the world—their way of thinking, writing, singing, reasoning, influencing. We must learn to speak in a language that the world understands. We must become viable conversation partners according to Craig Localzo.

5. Offer the proof of Christianity—the Resurrection (Acts 17:31).

    •   Paul spoke of the Resurrection. Christ's resurrection is the focal point of the faith, proving the central theme of Christianity. Without that fact we have no religion (1 Corinthians 15:13-14).

6. Make clear every person's accountability for his or her life (Acts 17:30-31).

    •   Paul didn't mince words. There comes a time when folks need to be told of a life audit.

7. Expect a variety of responses (Acts 17:5-9, 13, 18-20, 32-34).

    •   Paul received varied responses. Some will be jealous. Others will misrepresent what we are doing, accusing us of being troublemakers, agitating those we're trying to reach. But some will believe. And they are worth it!

Source Illumina Bible Software ©2002 Tyndale House Publishers www.tyndale.com

"Africa's fragility and conflict; the lingering impact of a colonial legacy of weak, inappropriate institutions; and the tremendous challenge of creating workable solutions on a continent grappling with such a profound diversity of political, cultural, linguistic, and religious identities. As many development partners have discovered, failure to understand the aforementioned factors goes hand in hand with failure to understand post-colonial state building efforts in Africa."

Source: Knowledge and Learning Unit Africa Capacity Building Foundation ©2011

We face very serious challenges in Africa and they are a result of a complexity of factors that affect how individuals build their lives and also how nations are built. Yet, these challenges are not insurmountable. On the contrary I believe Christians hold the destiny of Africa in their hearts as, "...treasure held within earthen vessels." to quote Paul in 2 Corinthians 4:7. Nothing is more exciting than seeing believers actively engaging the world they live in with God ideas.

Reflection Two

The Damming Effect
Implementing the God Idea

The Damming Effect is a cyclic knowledge based framework for planning and implementing ideas in a given context especially in developing and emerging nations. It is a metaphorical appreciation of the process in a dam that converts water to electricity. It constitutes 7 strategic steps that someone can take towards effectively implementing God's ideas.

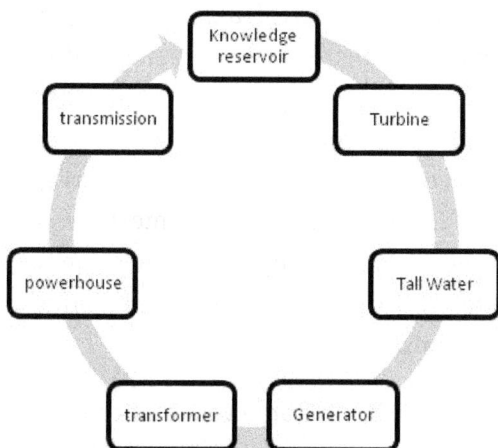

Figure 14 The Damming Effect

Developing nations are renowned for the most negative human conditions such as poverty, war and hunger.

More so in the continent of Africa, where the general perception is that, it is a continent bound by debilitating negative conditions that hinder development.

Yet, it is within these unbelievable situations that we find that unimaginable potential exists. The potential in developing nations can be likened to an unbridled torrential river flowing untamed, through a landscape. This potential is found in the people and is often left untapped.

It is natural and raw source of ideas and energy that can provide solutions for the basic necessities of life. It is often dangerous when misdirected and left unharnessed. Furthermore, it visibly has a small or subtle sphere of influence as long as it remains a river. If we probe deeper within the context of Africa's problems, we can discover emergent opportunities with immense torrential potential that can be harnessed to bring about transformation.

The Damming Effect is a framework that can contribute to systematic and knowledge based development initiatives that will subsequently bring about transformation and sustainable growth.

In an attempt to focus welfare interventions to local and integrated knowledge and skill, the Damming Effect provides a means to explore and discover the latent potential and innovation resident in the people. It is an opportunity for God ideas to collaborate with the existing cultural paradigm in a bid to effectively bring about transformation.

It builds on the premise that knowledge is obtained through understanding history (trends), appreciating the current (discontinuities), and considering the future (events and milestones).

I will present each step with a hypothetical case of how it can be applied in an organization or movement. In this case in a movement called The Art of Being Humane in their bid to raise awareness of cancer in Zimbabwe and advocating for more testing and screening in the country.

1) Knowledge Reservoir: the potential within

The Knowledge Reservoir represents the body of knowledge that is presently acquired, historic, present and futuristic. It is built upon the latent potential and inspiration of an individual and organization. It is the dam of unique attributes, experiences, skills and desire that shapes the current position, field of today and develops the seeds of tomorrow.

a) Through prayer and supplication the individual or organization develops an understanding of God's intentions for the present time and the future context.

b) The knowledge Reservoir also represents an opportunity for an individual or organization to appreciate and write down thoughts, reflections and key scriptures that emerge from the time of reflection.

c) Knowledge is often a shared resource; hence an individual or organization develops an appreciation of the knowledge and wisdom in other people and institutions. "There is wisdom in a multitude of counselors."

d) As knowledge gathers and key insights from key different counselors are recorded, a repository develops the clearly reflects what is required to fulfill God's mandate

e) In the midst of this process vision grows and imperatively a frontier (desired future path) for exploration emerges.

f) These become objectives and goals for the future that are fully aligned to God's intentions.

The Art of Being Humane started functioning by mining existing knowledge on cancer from local and international repositories and mixing it with the tacit and implied knowledge within their present movement of people. The movement proceeded to shape this knowledge into a vision in this case enabling the dissemination of information about cancer within the urban communities of Zimbabwe.

---

2) Turbine: releasing the potential within

The turbine is the active and kinetic pursuit of the future by matching plans and intentions to action within a context. It is momentum and inspiration drawn from knowledge acquired, an organization's or individual's competencies and the vision for the future. Transformational action can only be drawn out and effective when it arises out of matching thoughts of the future thought with present actions.

a) The turning turbine represents an opportunity to match objectives and goals with passions. This establishes the necessary underlying fuel that will sustain an individual or organization in the pursuit of a God idea.

b) The Turbine is also a process of alignment bridging the desired future, with day to day decisions and activities and the bigger and wider external context.

c) The turbine also presents an opportunity to explore the world around you.

d) Strategic reconnaissance (12 spies) represents the necessity and importance of analyzing and appreciating the emergent opportunities both medium and long term. When Moses sent out the 12 spies he gave them specific instructions,

   i) Observe what the land is like environment and potential.

   ii) Understand the people and their capacity and value systems.

   iii) Observe Cities and hubs or centres of activity

e) The turbine builds on this with more focused exploration of environment
   i) Events – the future will be affected by key events within your context e.g. political elections
   ii) Trends – an understanding of the cyclic occurrences within your market and community (fashion etc)
   iii) Discontinuities (big gaps and problems in the environment) – likely solutions that will change the way things will be done.

The turbine presents a process whereby the future becomes malleable as an individual or organization begins to match current activities, passions and vision with the future whilst exploring all possibilities pertaining to the future.

The Art of Being Humane started to match and align existing knowledge to their vision to disseminate cancer information to urban communities in Zimbabwe. Furthermore, the movement explored the context and tested their knowledge with existing collective knowledge and experience in the community. They came to the conclusion that they needed disseminate information among urban young adults were misinformed about the importance of getting tested.

3) Tall Water (Idea Recycler): sifting out potential

Tall water is a means to recycle and manage ideas (bad and good, necessary at the time and irrelevant). God ideas evolve and grow and thus need to constantly be challenged, tested and evaluated.

Idea recycling is another way of managing ideas. It is a part of the process that requires an appreciation of timing.

a) Evaluate your ideas and thoughts
b) Recycle ideas that cannot be applied
c) Analyze key insights relating to functional ideas
    i) Establish potential

The Art of being Humane came up with two ideas from the process. Firstly, to construct a cancer centre and secondly to start Tickled Pink Happy Hour Friday, relaxed contexts where people learn one fact about cancer. Tall water (idea Recycler) served as a tool to sift and evaluate ideas based on their viability in the near, medium and future term. Therefore the young movement at present couldn't afford to build a cancer center started Tickled Pink Happy Hour Friday. From hereon Construction of an Information Centre was set aside for further development in the idea management stream whilst Tickled Pink Happy Hour Friday became a viable idea that they are implementing.

4) Generator- creating opportunities

The generator represents the moments when an organization or individual can clearly see opportunities within the surrounding environment and how to convert these into a portfolio workable solutions.

a) Create a portfolio of opportunities
b) Evaluate ideas and match to community, market or situation.
  i) Recognize and assess key stakeholders
c) Recognize potential gaps and relevant discontinuities (creative disruptions)

> Once The Art of Being Humane had a clearer appreciation of the most practical and viable idea, the next step in the process was to develop the ideas further. The movement considered what practical actions it would take to make Tickled Pink Happy Hour Friday a consistent and thriving reality. At the same time the movement had other ideas in place like Blue Sport Saturdays (prostate cancer). Hence, they further categorized each idea according to size of project, cost, resources, time and so forth.

176

Transformation is a direct result of focused and purposeful action built on a new perspective. The transformer represents the moment when an individual or organization formulates strategic direction and the necessary actions to achieve the desired future.

a) Prepare a plan of action
b) Record key milestones and targets (goals)
c) Establish key strategic decisions and critical success factors
d) Map out potential network capital

> The Art of Being Humane Tickled Pink Happy Hour Friday along a critical path highlighting the key tasks that need to be fulfilled to ensure the success of the project.

6) *Powerhouse – investment and implementation*

Powerhouse represents the step focused on capacitating and facilitating the required resources and investment needed to ensure the project is launched successfully and sustainably over a period of time.

a) Mobilize available resources
b) Access networks
c) Garner relevant support from stakeholders

> The Art of Being Humane is presently a small movement today, but with the necessary financial, technical and human support it will be a bigger movement that ensures Zimbabwe and Africa become cancer free societies.

7) Transmission – learning from the community

Rather than antagonizing with a community, transmission allows for the smooth systematic flow of lessons and observations between your perceptions and the perceptions of the culture and context you're involved in and trying to initiate transformation. Therefore individuals or organizations become very relevant and effective messengers of the Gospel, learning as they teach.

a) Evaluation of feedback from the community
b) Establish knowledge gaps and performance indicators
c) Review key insights
d) Make strategic decision in response to feedback

In this case we assume that urban communities in the capital city are responding well to Tickled Pink Happy Hour Friday and appreciate the relaxed atmosphere created to teach a serious subject. Furthermore, they've requested that Tickled Pink Happy Hour Friday celebrate one person who has survived cancer and how they've done it. Also that once a month Pink Friday and Blue Saturday come together for combined talk on healthy living. The movement mines this data and processes it until it becomes implementable knowledge in the reservoir (step 1) and proceeds to start the damming effect once more.

Knowledge Reservoir	Art of Being Humane starts a cancer awareness initiative in Zimbabwe
Turbine	Art of Being Humane aligns objectives to their vision and explore the impact of cancer in the community.
Tall Water	Manage ideas (build information centre or start to Tickled Pink Happy Hour Friday)
Generator	Plan and Consider resources needed to make to Tickled Pink Happy Hour Friday a success.
Transformer	Map out to Tickled Pink Happy Hour Friday along a critical path. Gather info on cancer and start @venue e.g. Freshly Ground.
Powerhouse	Implement in community/recreation centres around the city. And initiate networks for investment.
Transmission	Learn from sessions and adjust to Tickled Pink Happy Hour Friday accordingly.

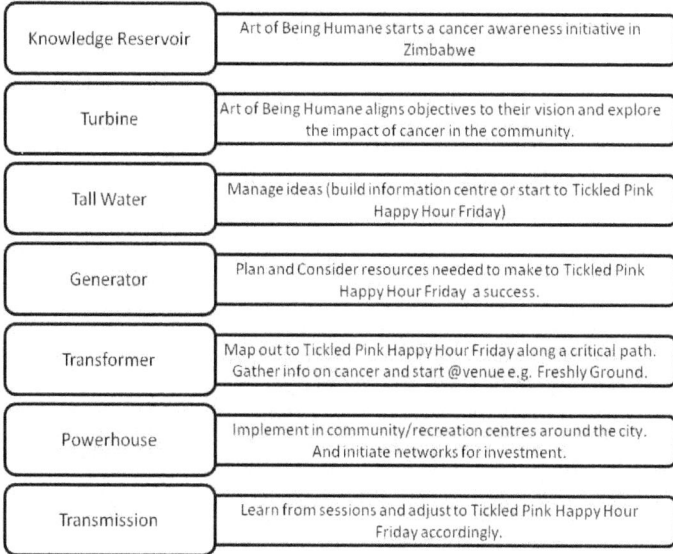

Figure 15. Summary Damming Effect

Reflection Three

God ideas shaping the future

How possible is it to help shape the transformational future as presented to us in the Word of God? Considering that the rule and reign of God (Kingdom) is both present tense that is, we experience the effect of God's intentions at present and it is future tense, meaning that it is yet to come. I believe it is very possible. Importantly, believers must embrace the responsibility and yoke that Jesus asks us to carry.

Our main responsibility as believers is to preach the good news of the Kingdom of God (His rule and reign) to the ends of the earth. The other aspect of our responsibility is to do what the word says. This can be achieved as;

- We create a narrative and establish the driving forces of the future.
  - What and who is driving the future of our lives, communities and nations?
- Identify predetermined factors that are inevitable of the future
  - What key factors affect the future of human history? E.g. the second coming of the Lord Jesus Christ. And the truth that He has died for all sins.

- Help individuals and communities to assess areas of uncertainty.
    o "You do not know the day or the hour..."
- We must help believers create a series of strategies and alternatives.
- Help believers assess implications of different scenarios.
    o "With the increase of wickedness the love of many will grow cold..." Matt 24:12. How does this affect Christian ministry in the future?
- Identify and monitor key indicators to allow believes to continue assessing the impact of a God Idea.

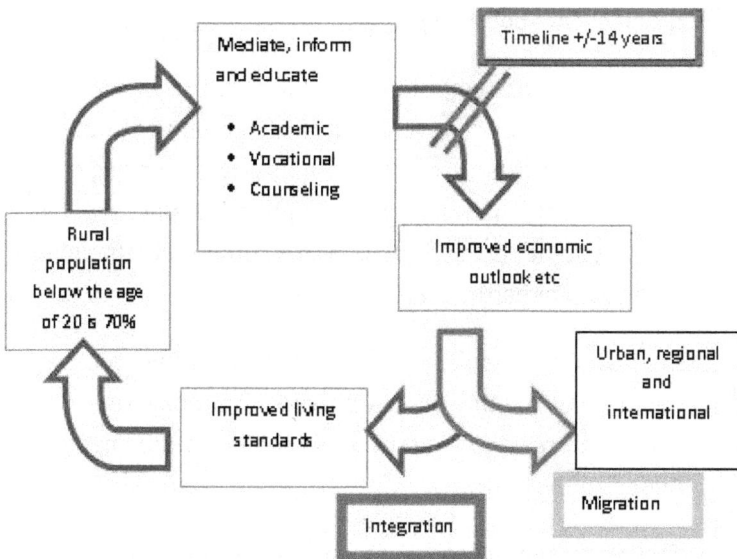

Figure 16: Systematic approach to development

The diagram above (Figure 16) reveals a cycle of decisions and actions that lead to transformation. In the example above consideration is given that a significant percentage of a rural community's population (i.e. 70%) is below the age of 20.

Through acts of compassion and a desire to support the development and growth of an impoverished rural community, individuals called by God respond appropriately to the need. What will be evident is firstly a need to mediate. Isaiah refers to this as, repairing the breach. These individuals bring the good news to the poor in a bid and intent desire to make disciples (not converts).

This means that what happens for a period of time is, these individuals seek to affect this community through dedicated efforts to inform them of wrong thinking and to educate them. It isn't an overnight missionary activity but a genuine response of love to a community that will take years of hard work.

Over time the results will become clearer as we see the community with an improved outlook on life (furthermore and importantly seeing more people added to the faith).

The community becomes more dynamic and mobile and soon we'll find that two things happen. Firstly, there will be those who will migrate and seek to be relevant in another prescribed context such as urban areas or other countries. The second response becomes important to the rural community.

We find these are 'discipled' people who integrate, that is to say they actively and constructively become a transformational part of the community.

This will only result in a significant change in living standards and values and the cycle of transformation towards glorifying God continues and then generation upon generation experience the impact and influence of God ideas.

Examples of activities

1. Building new or restoring old amenities and infrastructure, like schools, clinics, boreholes and so forth.
2. Educating families and communities through schools and other vocational training initiatives.
3. Empowering communities financially and socially to be more productive through the development and fostering of enterprise.
4. Teaching and advocating for stewardship. Missionary activities or interventions should focus on restoring human responsibility for certain consequences like poverty. This also implies teaching communities to save and invest. This presents one of the most powerful interventions. It is, when a community values what they have been given by God and makes use of it responsibly for the good of the whole community.

5. Learning in a community must go beyond being rote (habitual) to practical and iterative appreciation.
6. Advocating for healthier links between a community and other communities (external donors).

ARK (Art Reach Kids)

In Zimbabwe there's an organization working with orphans and vulnerable children called ARK (Art Reach Kids). Their vision is to inspire creativity, passion and joy.

By actively seeking to raise children's self concept, ARK is systematically using art to mediate, inform and educate children. This will ultimately build their self esteem, communication skills and social skills.

If ARK continues this process over a certain period (e.g.10years), the eventual result will be the transformation of a community.

Already among the 20 children they work with in an orphanage in Harare, art is proving a very powerful tool to help orphans improve their outlook of the future socially and economically.

Eventually, these orphans will have the capacity to either migrate or integrate as agents of transformation wherever they are.

What began as a God idea in an individual, is already shaping the future of 20 young orphans and will eventually shape the future of countless orphaned and vulnerable children in Zimbabwe, Africa and the world.

Reflection four

Views of Life

There are four views I would like to present to us which I believe will always be a part of human existence.

In our lives we will be,

1. In the valley
2. Standing on a cliff
3. Standing atop a peak
4. And soaring like an eagle

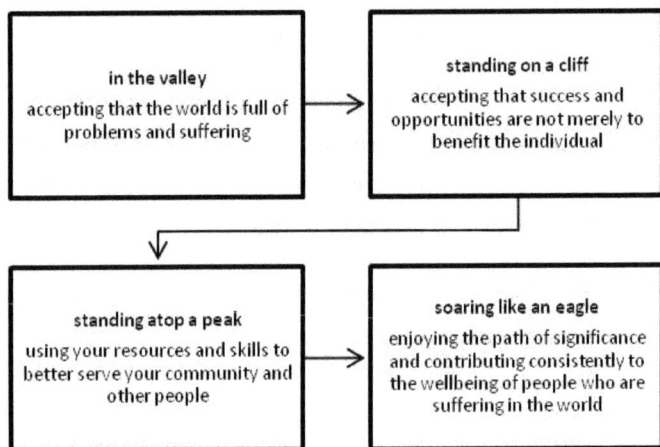

```
┌─────────────────────────────┐       ┌─────────────────────────────┐
│        in the valley        │       │     standing on a cliff     │
│  accepting that the world   │  ──▶  │   accepting that success    │
│  is full of problems and    │       │   and opportunities are     │
│         suffering           │       │   not merely to benefit     │
│                             │       │      the individual         │
└─────────────────────────────┘       └─────────────────────────────┘
              │                                        │
              ▼                                        │
┌─────────────────────────────┐       ┌─────────────────────────────┐
│     standing atop a peak    │       │    soaring like an eagle    │
│  using your resources and   │  ──▶  │  enjoying the path of       │
│  skills to better serve     │       │  significance and           │
│  your community and other   │       │  contributing consistently  │
│          people             │       │  to the wellbeing of people │
│                             │       │  who are suffering in the   │
│                             │       │           world             │
└─────────────────────────────┘       └─────────────────────────────┘
```

Figure 17 Views of Life

For a different section of us, life may potentially be lived permanently in one of these four states more specifically most of us will live in the first 2, whilst never really enjoying what it means to become significant so as to soar.

The reason I believe this is simply put in a few synonymous words like, empathy, love, compassion and mercy. Much of what we'll do in life is based on satisfying the objects of our affection, namely self. Much of our frustration and vainglory will come from either losing out on what we thought we deserved or attaining to the transient success we believed would bring us happiness.

Until we appreciate that our world needs more love and empathy, we will constantly be caught up in the cycle of being in the valley of disappointment and suffering and the cliff of transient achievement. We will be left with an elusive hope to ascend upwards towards significance so that one day we would soar.

View1: The Valley

Psa 23

"Though I walk through the valley of the shadow of death I shall fear no evil for your rod and staff they comfort me." RSV

The valley represents much of what every human being will inevitably endure at some point in their lives. We will all face loss and be faced with the need to endure suffering and pain.

No one in this world is exempt from pain and suffering. In truth it can be said that most of us will face suffering daily. It is in the valley that many lessons will be learned or ignored.

The valley constitutes moments one can be termed the underling who no one really cares for. Some people relate to the valley more than others (possibly those born into privilege). Yet, everybody in the world will endure some sort of anguish. It is in this state that we must learn and understand the power of empathy.

As we consider and ponder our state of suffering, the lesson to be learned is that someone else somewhere else in the world is enduring the same or facing less or worse. In our state of anguish and despair, as hard as it sounds to think about another person, it is somehow imperative to understand that suffering and hardship are commonplace to most people; it's just that others hide it better than some.

Rich people hide behind wealth and excess, successful people hide behind over exertion and an ambitious quest to be better than they already are. Yet, for all of us we will encounter valley moments and it is here that we must draw on the Lord and see something glorious (that we have beautiful feet that carry the good news).

Answer the following questions

1. What kind of loss and suffering have you endured in your life?
2. How have you responded to that suffering?
3. Have you learned anything from the suffering you faced? What has God taught you through that suffering?
4. Do you know anyone else who is suffering or going through loss?
5. What is the foundation of true freedom and happiness in your life?

View 2: The Cliff

Once in a place of suffering and hardship we may come across good fortune through hard work or time and chance. We find ourselves in a better place in every manner of speaking. It is here that many of us sojourn and then tarry more permanently.

We lose sight of the greater call and good, we get choked by the cares of the world and become mongers of self actualization, preservation and anything else that will temporarily satisfy the gnawing sense that there is more to life than the success we have obtained.

As we build tents and dwell in our success we can lose sight of the world around us and often lose sight to the needs of our fellow man. Our sense of brotherhood is monetized and valued according to a small cheque or donation.

We can also potentially discover the person (Samaritan) who will expend more than a small donation to someone starving somewhere across the world due to some natural disaster or a war created by greedy men.

As we stand on the cliff, there must be a recollection of times when we have suffered and endured pain or loss. This recollection serves as a reminder to us that the reality of this world intimates that someone somewhere is in need of our help.

Someone somewhere needs more than a plate of porridge coming from a kind donation. I'm not saying that donating money is a bad thing or a sign of a lack of compassion.

Rather, that we are in a privileged place where we can do and give more as believers. Once we understand that everybody is looking for love, we are able to look around us and see the drug addict, the prostitute, the beggar, the widows and orphans and anybody else faced with a crisis in their lives. Thereby we are then able to extend not just a helping hand but an open ear and a compassionate heart.

The challenge for us is that in our success we need to look around and see some of the problems and crises that other people are facing and recognize them as opportunities to make a difference.

It is this extension that gradually leads to a clearer glimpse that our material success and achievement is simply a cliff protruding from a large mountain and that there is something higher to attain to...

Questions to ask and answer
1. Do you have any success in you life?
2. What does that success mean to you?
3. How does you success affect your family and community?
4. Do you recognize other people in need? Can you see some problems in your community? How do those problems make you feel?
5. Is there anything you would want to do about it?

View 3: Standing atop a peak

As we extend that hand of compassion and love, we are certain to get a greater glimpse of the meaning of our lives. The peak of our existence and actualization will only arise when we love our neighbor as we love ourselves.

Our neighbor may be the person we think is immoral and only deserves death, they maybe a person who has no other chance in life other than living in a constant state of fear faced by a ravaging war.

Standing atop a peak, gives us a panoramic view of life and the realities therein and a lease of life that tells us, that we can rise above life's circumstances and make a difference.

From the peak we are able to see the world as it is, a place though filled with pain and suffering that still carries a sense of beauty and love. It is this vision of the world that will birth a deeper sense of purpose and significance within us as we realize that we are vessels and conduits of God's unfailing and unconditional love.

Our significance is based on Jesus' commandment to love our neighbor as we love ourselves. We can attain obscene amounts of wealth, ascend the cliffs of success but without a deeper sense of purpose that serves our fellow man we can never truly enjoy significance, the realization and experience of living the life that God called us to.

Questions to answer

1. How can you begin to help someone change their lives? Or how can you help to change or solve some of the problems in your community?
2. How can you use your God given abilities to make a difference someone's life?
3. Try to list 5 ways that your insight has changed and how you will pass on the knowledge to someone else searching for significance

View 4: Soaring

The eagle can easily be considered an arrogant creature as it soars high up in the sky; so too the man or woman seen to be doing so much for the community. But I believe that the eagle is courageous and confident. So too I believe the people pursuing and walking the path of significance. They are people who are courageous and confident.

People who are significant, who carry the compassion to make a difference and serve other people will naturally be inclined to soar. There is a Native America story told, that an eagle doesn't fly away from the storm; rather it flies into the storm.

Once in the storm, the eagle uses the convection waves to rise above the storm. Nothing more can be true about a man or woman who isn't content with life *(the status quo)* and passionately seeks to serve and love other people and the community at large; they naturally rise above the storms (problems) of life.

1. What does the verse, "I came that you might have life and life in abundance." (John 10:10b RSV) mean to you?
2. How do you believe you can really enjoy the life that God has given you?
3. If your life was absolutely perfect what would it look like?
4. What do you want to be remembered for?

Think about what George Bernard Shaw a famous writer once said, "This is the true joy in my life-the being used for a purpose recognized by yourself as a mighty one, the being a force of nature instead of feverish, selfish little clod of ailments and grievances, complaining that the world will not devote itself to making your happy.

I am of the opinion that my life belongs to the whole community and as long as I live, it is my privilege to do for it whatever I can. I want to be thoroughly used up when I die, for the harder I work, the more I live. I rejoice in life for its own sake.

Life is no brief candle to me. It is a sort of splendid torch which I've got ahold of for the moment, and I want to make it burn as brightly as possible before handing it on to future generations."

Summary of Keys

1. Ideas form the basis of all human endeavours. Someone somewhere conceived something and sought to make it a reality.
2. We are uniquely created by God to subdue the earth.
3. Human beings have the capacity and intelligence to invent.
4. God selects individuals to do His work by name.
5. Bezalel was filled with the Spirit of God.
6. Obedience means responding to God's instruction, even when it doesn't seem to make sense.
7. Courageously believing in the dreams God gives us, is a key ingredient to establishing God ideas.
8. Obeying God's instruction, leads to ideas that make an impact on future generations.
9. Learn to keep a God idea a secret until the appointed time to impart the vision.
10. People will recognize and acknowledge an excellent spirit in you.
11. God ideas affect the politics of men, and government structures of nations.
12. God ideas can reflect the wisdom of God in different disciplines.
13. True wisdom is found in and with God.
14. God's wisdom is revealed in the death and resurrection of Christ Jesus.
15. God's creative power (Bara) is the cornerstone all God Ideas.
16. God is actively involved in His creation, especially man.
17. The Gospel is more than just words and works it's God's ability to shape all levels of society.

18. All believers are an expression of God's handiwork.
19. God expresses His love through the actions of believers.
20. God ideas revive all areas of society
21. The Word of God renews our thinking and logic.
22. Problems and challenges are opportunities to reveal God ideas.
23. We are called to affect society wit God Ideas
24. The saving grace is a practical tool for transformation.
25. We are unique representatives of God's intentions on earth.
26. God ideas express and display God's glory to the world.
27. We can draw on God's wisdom for every aspect of life.
28. We need to live by design, with the end in mind.

Works Cited and Bibliography

Barclay, W. 1971, Ethics in a permissive society, Collins Clear Type Press Fontana Books, Great Britain.

Barclay, W. 1973, The Gospel of Luke *The Daily Study Bible,* The Saint Andrew Press, Edinburgh, Scotland.

Biblesoft's New Exhaustive Strong's Numbers and Concordance with Expanded Greek-Hebrew Dictionary. Copyright © 1994, 2003, 2006 Biblesoft, Inc. and International Bible Translators, Inc.)

Buford, B. 1994, Half Time, Zondervan Press , Michigan, USA.

Chambers, O. 1912, Biblical Psycology, Partridge and Co, London, England

Clark, D. 2007, Forgotten Fundamentals, Cedar Fort Inc, Springville, USA

Concise Oxford Dictionary © 2001, Oxford University Press, Oxford, UK.

De Bono, E. 1982, Lateral Thinking for Management, Pelican Books, Great Britain

Glover, T.R. 1944, The Ancient World, Pelican Books, Great Britain

Grudem, W. 1999, Bible Doctrine, InterVarsity Press, England.

Grudem, W. 2003, Business for the Glory of God, Crossway Books, Illinois, USA.

Hadas, M., 1965, Imperial Rome, *Great Ages of Man,* Time Inc, USA

Hill, N., 1938, Think and Grow Rich, The Ralston Society, Meriden, Connecticut, USA

Holy Bible *Amplified Version, 1987,* Lackerman Foundation, Zondervan Publishing, USA.

Holy Bible New International Version® NIV® 1978, New York International Bible Society.

Illumina Bible Software ©2002 Tyndale House Publishers www.tyndale.com.

Jamieson, Fausset, and Brown Commentary, Electronic Database. Copyright © 1997, 2003, 2005, 2006 by Biblesoft, Inc. All rights reserved.)

Keller Tim, 2010, Live in Johannesburg notes, South Africa.

Knowledge and Learning Unit Africa Capacity Building Foundation ©2011.

Lewis, C.S. Mere Christianity, 1961 Fontana Books, Collins Prints, Great Britain.

Liesch, B. Dr, 1999 Creativity Sacramentalist View, www.worshipinfo.com/materials/creativity.html

Localzo, C. A., 2000, Apologetic Preaching, InterVarsity Press, USA

Mangawalwadi R&V, 1997, William Carey and the Regeneration of India, Nivedit Good Books, USA

Miller, D. *et al* 2005, God's Remarkable Plan for the nations, Youth with a Mission Publishing, Seattle, USA.

Miller, D. *et al* 2005, God's Unshakeable Kingdom, Youth with a Mission Publishing, Seattle, USA.

Miller, D. *et al* 2005, The Worldview of the Kingdom of God, Youth with a Mission Publishing, Seattle, USA.

Mises, L. 2006, Economic Policy *thoughts for today and tomorrow,* Ludwig Von Mises Institute, Alabama, USA

Sherwood, D., 2002b, Innovation Express, Capstone

Walsh, J.B. and Middleton, R.J. 1984, The Transforming Vision, *Shaping a Christian World View,* Intervarsity Christian Fellowship of the United States.

Walvoord J. and Zuck R. ©1983, 2004 The Bible Knowledge Commentary: Old Testament by David C Cook. USA

Van Wyk Hein, 2006, Hope for Africa, transformation through local church, Viva Network Zimbabwe.

About the book

Ideas have shaped the history of humanity. Ideas are shaping the present. Ideas will shape the future. From technology, economics and even in the realm of politics, at the core of our livelihoods ideas are foundational.

The author was convicted by God that creativity and innovation cannot be an autonomous and untrammeled human endeavour but, must rightly originate from the source of all things. The God Idea is a book designed to highlight the effect of God's intentions in the societies we live in.

It is upon this premise that this book explores what the author calls the God Idea. What ideas does God have concerning human existence? What ideas does God have for your life? Open this book and discover the God idea in you.